The MAILBOX®

grades 3–5

D1277891

Black History

The MAILBOX® MAGAZINE

The best activities and reproducibles from past issues of *The Mailbox*® and *Teacher's Helper*® magazines

Highlight black history throughout your curriculum with

- ### Reading comprehension passages
- ### Vocabulary extenders
- ### Writing prompts and ideas
- ### Math activities
- ### Student projects and more!

Use the index on page 80 to locate specific Black American achievers.

Managing Editor: Jenny Chapman

Editorial Team: Becky S. Andrews, Diane Badden, Kimberley Bruck, Karen A. Brudnak, Kitty Campbell, Lynette Dickerson, Sarah Foreman, Theresa Lewis Goode, Tazmen Hansen, Marsha Heim, Lori Z. Henry, Debra Liverman, Dorothy C. McKinney, Thad H. McLaurin, Sharon Murphy, Jennifer Nunn, Mark Rainey, Hope Rodgers

www.themailbox.com

©2008 The Mailbox®
All rights reserved.
ISBN10 #1-56234-852-3 • ISBN13 #978-156234-852-6

Manufactured in the United States
10 9 8 7 6 5 4 3 2 1

Table of Contents

Language Arts and Math:
Skills Overview 3

Harriet Tubman and the
Underground Railroad 4

A Man and His Dream:
Martin Luther King Jr. 10

Black History Month 29

Artist Extraordinaire:
Meet Romare Bearden 42

Leading the Way: Contemporary
Black American Achievers 43

Black History Month by the Numbers 46

Additional Student Practice Pages 50

Answer Keys 75

Index of Black American Achievers 80

Language Arts and Math
Skills Overview

Language Arts

conventions

    quotations, 23

grammar

    adverbs, 73

    past-tense verbs, 22

literature

    responding to, 4, 5, 6, 7, 10

reading

    comprehension, 9, 20, 52–53, 55–56, 59–60, 61–62, 65–66, 67–68, 69

    context clues, 63

    critical thinking, 27, 52–53, 74

    fact and opinion, 21

    following directions, 24

    inferences, 64

    prior knowledge, 43, 45

    recalling details, 4, 5, 17

    recalling facts, 29, 32, 33, 40, 41, 45

    sequencing, 10, 19, 28, 51

    supporting details, 18

    synonyms, 57

    topic sentence, 18

reasoning

    deductive, 71

research

    skills, 29, 31, 33, 38, 39, 70

vocabulary

    content, 8

writing

    captions, 5, 13

    descriptive, 38

    letters, 37

    lists, 36, 37

    opinion, 35, 36, 37, 58

    paragraphs, 13, 27, 30, 35, 37, 44

    persuasive, 38

    poetry, 30, 34, 35

    prompts, 11, 12, 15, 35, 36, 37, 38

    proofreading, 54

    sentences, 11, 12, 14, 16, 44

    summary, 10, 12, 43

Math

algebra

    ordered pairs, 47, 72

measurement

    converting units of measure, 49

numbers and operations

    computation, 24

    division, 26

    equivalent fractions, 25

    mixed numbers, 25

    multiplication, 48

Harriet Tubman and the Underground Railroad

Former slave Harriet Tubman became the driving force of the Underground Railroad—a network of hiding places and forest trails that led slaves to free northern states and eventually into Canada. There were no rails for the runaways to follow, just the North Star and plenty of tracks and trails. Along the way an occasional lantern or quilt signaled a house where safety, shelter, and food awaited them.

by Njeri Jones and Deborah Zink Roffino

Minty: A Story Of Young Harriet Tubman

Written by Alan Schroeder & Illustrated by Jerry Pinkney

Tender and emotional watercolor illustrations introduce readers to Minty, a spunky and headstrong eight-year-old who holds a special dream tucked inside her heart. For Harriet Tubman's own escape from slavery, and to engineer the freedom of so many others, she needed ingenuity and countless survival skills. This fictional account of her childhood, which is based on extensive research, suggests ways she may have acquired the skills she needed to free herself, and hundreds of others, from slavery.

It took many years before Minty's dream came true, but she never gave up! Minty was about 29 years old and known as Harriet Tubman when she finally made her daring escape from the Brodas plantation. Share this information at the conclusion of the book; then draw the outline of a large sunflower on the board. Remind students how Minty pretended to be a sunflower when no one was looking. Then use the sunflower sketch to show students how Minty kept her dream alive for all those years. To do this, write Minty's wish—"To Escape!"—in the flower center. Next ask students to recall ways that Minty worked toward her dream. Write these ideas on the petals. When each petal is programmed, help students understand that working toward a dream is the best way to make it come true. Then have each child draw an outline of a large sunflower on a 12" x 18" sheet of drawing paper. Ask each child to write his dream in the center of the flower, how he is working toward the dream in the flower petals, and his name inside a leaf outline. Suggest that each student use crayons to outline his drawing and create desired background scenery. Display the projects on a bulletin board titled "Our Field Of Dreams!"

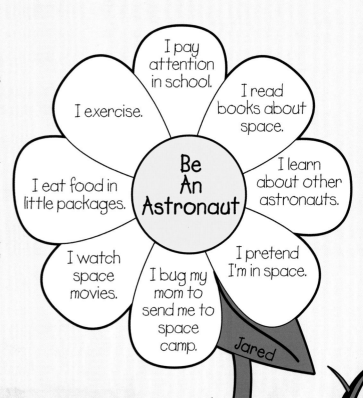

Barefoot: Escape On The Underground Railroad

Written by Pamela Duncan Edwards
Illustrated by Henry Cole

Near the floor of the deep, dark woods, the bare feet of a young man creep softly in a desperate move toward freedom. On this stretch of the Underground Railroad, Barefoot trusts only the sounds of woodland creatures to assist his flight. The croak of a frog means water is near; the cry of a heron echoes danger. Dark and powerful illustrations create a shadowy nighttime world that is filled with fear and uncertainty.

After an initial oral reading of the story, have students recall the things that Barefoot hears as he presses forward along the Underground Railroad. List these items on the board. Then read the story aloud a second time so students can listen carefully for additional sound makers. Make any needed additions to the class list, and with your youngsters' help, assign a sound effect to each listed item. Next, under your direction, have the class practice each sound effect. Before each sound is made, ask students how hearing that sound on the trail might have made Barefoot feel. Then encourage students to incorporate these feelings into their sound renditions. Finally read the story aloud one more time, this time arranging for a different small group of students to make each sound effect on the list. This journey along the Underground Railroad will leave a lasting impression!

Item	Sound Effect
Barefoot's breath	*(three heavy breaths)*
heron	"skreeeeek, skreeeeek"
Heavy Boots	*(stomp feet three times)*
frog	"ribbit, ribbit, ribbit"
mouse	"nibble, nibble, nibble"
mockingbird	"tra la la, tra la la"
squirrel	"scamper, scamper, scamper"
deer	*(crumpling of paper)*
mosquitoes	"buzz, buzz, buzz"
fireflies	"zing, zing, zing"

Aunt Harriet's Underground Railroad In The Sky

Written & Illustrated by Faith Ringgold

Ringgold's celebrated folk art takes readers to the skies for an imaginative blend of fact and fantasy. Flying high among the stars, Cassie and her brother Be Be learn about the Underground Railroad and discover why Black American slaves were willing to risk their lives for freedom. The dream sequence, which is conducted by Harriet Tubman herself, is based on Tubman's dream of flying to freedom.

At the conclusion of this story, ask students to recall events from Cassie's trip on the Underground Railroad. Encourage students to tell what they learned about slavery, Harriet Tubman, and the series of trails and hiding places called the Underground Railroad. Then, in celebration of the Underground Railroad and the freedom that it brought to hundreds of slaves, have your students create a class Freedom Train. First ask students to brainstorm symbols of freedom and describe benefits of living in a free country. List the students' ideas on the board. Then ask each child to choose one idea from the list to illustrate and write a brief caption about it on a 9" x 12" sheet of drawing paper. Next have each child trim two 3-inch squares of black construction paper into circles and glue the resulting train wheels near the bottom of his project. Display the train cars, connected by 1" x 4" strips of black paper (hitches), along a classroom wall. Add engine and caboose cutouts, and this freedom train is ready to spread the word about liberty and justice for all!

Allen Jay And The Underground Railroad
Written by Marlene Targ Brill
Illustrated by Janice Lee Porter

When his father is unable to help, young Allen Jay finds the courage to aid a runaway slave. His family's farm is a stop on the Underground Railroad, and the boy's parents, who are Quakers, are secret conductors. It is 11-year-old Allen Jay's first experience as a conductor. The clearly written narrative, seen through the eyes of the heroic young Quaker boy, is based on actual events of the 1840s. Muted pastel illustrations accentuate Allen Jay's gripping story.

Conductors of the Underground Railroad risked their lives to help others whom they felt were being treated unfairly. At the conclusion of this story, have students contemplate the courage that Allen Jay displayed to lend a helping hand to Henry. Also ask students to express feelings Allen Jay may have felt as he shook Henry's hand and wished him a safe trip to Canada. Encourage your youngsters to practice helpful behavior with this follow-up activity. Ask each child to trace the shape of his hand on a sheet of drawing paper, then cut out the resulting shape and label it with his name. Each time a child lends a helping hand throughout the day, he collects the signature of the person whom he helped. At the end of the day he will have a visual reminder of his helpful ways. Before dismissal, invite student volunteers to talk about how it feels knowing that they have helped others that day.

Sweet Clara And The Freedom Quilt
Written by Deborah Hopkinson
Illustrated by James Ransome

Based on a true little-known chapter of black history, this powerful picture book tells the story of a young slave girl's plan to map the route of the Underground Railroad. When her last stitch is in place, Sweet Clara has hidden in the squares of her quilt the path that will guide her and many other slaves to freedom. Brightly colored full-page paintings light up the pages of this inspirational tale.

Clara stitches her dreams for the future into a quilt that helps her and others. After reading the story to students and discussing it with them, ask each child to think of a dream that he has for the future that others will benefit from as well. Then have each student illustrate his dream on a six-inch square of white construction paper. Next have each child glue his artwork in the center of an eight-inch square of colorful construction paper that you have punched with a series of equally spaced holes—four per side. To assemble the quilt, divide students into groups of four. Give each group four 1-foot lengths of yarn to use to stitch the group's projects into one large square. Provide assistance as needed. Then have one student from each group volunteer to help stitch the resulting projects into a desired quilt shape. Display the completed quilt for all to see. Ask each child to reveal which quilt patch he designed and talk about his dream for the future.

More Books About Harriet Tubman

A Picture Book Of Harriet Tubman

Written by David A. Adler & Illustrated by Samuel Byrd

Born more than forty years before the Civil War, Harriet Tubman possessed a powerful love for her people and for freedom. This biography touches upon her years as a slave, her perilous escape, her numerous trips as a conductor on the Underground Railroad, and her duties as a nurse during the Civil War. Readers also learn of Harriet's work after the war, which included helping to establish a home in New York State for impoverished Black Americans. Memorable acrylic paintings accent the highlights of Harriet's ninety-plus years.

Harriet Tubman
A Photo-Illustrated Biography

Written by Margo McLoone

Divided into 9 one-page chapters, each with an accompanying full-page black-and-white photograph, this beginner's biography is perfect for the primary classroom. After a brief introduction to the brave conductor, readers are presented with an overview of Tubman's life that focuses on key events and accomplishments. The final page of the book features a brief bibliography, useful addresses, Internet sites, and an index.

Your youngsters will warm right up to this quilt-making project! Remind students that a quilt displayed outside a home signaled to slaves traveling along the Underground Railroad that the home was safe to approach. Then ask each child to design a precut quilt patch for a class freedom quilt. Explain that this quilt will signal to others that your classroom is a safe place for *all* people. Mount the quilt patches and a title patch on a bulletin board covered with colorful paper. Then use a marker to draw stitch lines between the projects.

An Amazing Woman

Read.
Write a word from each sentence in the puzzle.
(Hint: Only one word will fit.)

1. My parents were slaves.
2. I was born a slave.
3. My name was Araminta.
4. My family called me Minty.
5. Being a slave was very hard work.
6. At night I listened to stories of freedom.
7. I learned about the Underground Railroad.
8. My dream was to escape.
9. I was an adult when I escaped to freedom.
10. I was so thankful to be free!
11. I helped many other slaves find freedom.
12. I kept helping people for the rest of my life.

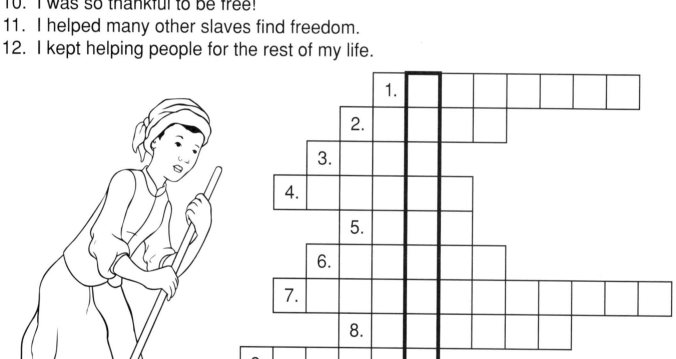

Harriet Tubman was the first African American woman to be pictured on this.
What is it? (Hint: Study the puzzle from top to bottom.)

___ ___ ___ ___ ___ ___   ___ ___ ___ ___ ___

Escape To Freedom
Harriet Tubman
(1820?–1913)

As a young slave growing up on a Maryland plantation, Harriet Tubman was known for her independent spirit. She would not pretend to be polite and eager to please her masters just so that she could get an easier job as a house slave. Instead she preferred the harder work in the fields where she could be in the sunshine and fresh air. Never pretending to be satisfied with her life as a slave, Harriet could not be forced to smile while she worked. Once Harriet even risked her own life to protect a runaway slave from his overseer's whip.

When Harriet was older, she ran away from the plantation to go to the North. In the North there was no slavery and Harriet could be free. During the years that followed, Harriet became an important member of the Underground Railroad. The Underground Railroad was a system for helping slaves escape to freedom. She repeatedly returned to Maryland to "conduct," or lead, escaping slaves on a safe route to the North. It was always a very dangerous job. There was even a $40,000 bounty for anyone who captured Harriet! But Harriet was never caught and never lost a "passenger" on the Underground Railroad. In all, she helped over 300 slaves, including her parents, escape from slavery.

Answer the following questions. Use the back of this page if you need more space.

1. List evidence from the story that proves that Harriet was an independent young girl.

   _____

   _____

2. How did Harriet fight against slavery when she was older? _____

   _____

   _____

3. What was the Underground Railroad?_____

   _____

4. What personal characteristics do you think Harriet possessed in order to do what she did to fight slavery? _____

   _____

5. Why do you think that Harriet was willing to make such dangerous trips back to the South to help other slaves escape? _____

   _____

   _____

6. If you had lived in Harriet's time, how would you have fought against slavery? _____

   _____

A Man and His Dream

Use these engaging activities to teach students about a remarkable American who dreamed that one day there would be peace and justice for all.

Martin Luther King Jr.

Provide students with a snapshot of the boyhood, adult life, and dreams of Martin Luther King Jr. by reading aloud one of the following books:

Happy Birthday, Martin Luther King • Written by Jean Marzollo • Illustrated by J. Brian Pinkney
A Picture Book of Martin Luther King, Jr. • Written by David A. Adler • Illustrated by Robert Casilla

Speaking Out

Dr. King felt that it was his responsibility, or duty, to speak out against violence. Ask students why they think he felt this way. Help them understand that the safety and well-being of the world is everyone's responsibility, and that every person can contribute to making a positive difference. Invite students to share any concerns they have about the world. List their ideas on the board. Then ask each child to choose one concern from the list and design a poster that speaks out against it. Remind students that when Dr. King spoke out, he always provided peaceful solutions. Ask students to do the same. After each child has presented his poster to the class, showcase the messages around the school.

Festive Timelines

In celebration of Dr. King's birthday (the third Monday in January), have each child make a festive four-event timeline of his life. To make a timeline, fold a 3" x 12" strip of drawing paper in half twice; then unfold the paper to reveal four equal sections. Leaving a half-inch margin at the top of the strip and working in chronological order from left to right, label each section with a different event.

To transform the project into a birthday cake look-alike, accordion-fold the strip and decorate the front of the folded project to resemble a birthday cake. Next cut out four candle flames from scrap paper and glue them to the tops of four ½" x 2" construction paper strips to make lit candles. Unfold the timeline and glue one candle to the top of each section, positioning the candles so that when the project is refolded, each one is visible.

Happy Birthday, Dr. King!

In 1929 Martin Luther King Jr. was born in Atlanta, Georgia.

In 1953 Martin got married to Coretta Scott.

In 1963 he gave a speech in Washington, DC, about his dream for the future.

In 1964 Martin Luther King Jr. won the Nobel Peace Prize.

Gifts of Peace

Martin Luther King Jr. dreamed of the day when all people could live in peace. Invite students to describe what *peace* means to them. Encourage plenty of discussion and accept all answers. Then, on provided paper, have each child describe and illustrate one gift of peace that she would give the world. Invite each child to share her gift with the class. Then collect the papers and publish them in a class book titled "Our Gifts of Peace."

Our Gifts of Peace

I would give the gift of listening to one another.

Sherry

Footsteps to Follow

When Martin Luther King Jr. graduated from college, he decided to become a minister just like his father. Explain to students that because Martin admired his father so much, he was proud to follow in his footsteps. Ask each student to label a colorful footprint pattern with the name of a person she admires and hopes to grow up to be like. After she cuts out the pattern, have her copy, complete, and illustrate the sentence "When I am older I hope to follow in the footsteps of [name or description of person] because..." Display the completed projects on a bulletin board titled "Footsteps We Hope to Follow."

Grandpa Keller

When I am older I hope to follow in the footsteps of Grandpa Keller because he helps sick kids. He is a doctor.

Keeping the Dream Alive

Dr. King's dream included freedom, peace, and understanding. He dreamed that one day all people would love and help each other. Review Dr. King's dream with the class and challenge students to explain how they can contribute to keeping it alive. Help them realize the impact that their thoughts and actions have on his dream. Next give each child a copy of page 14 and a 6" x 18" strip of red or blue construction paper. To complete the project, a child writes an ending for each sentence and colors the portrait of Dr. King. Then he cuts along the bold lines, positions the pieces on his construction paper in a pleasing manner, and glues them in place. If desired, have each child hole-punch the top of his project, thread a length of curling ribbon through the holes, and tie the ribbon ends. Suggest that each child display his project at home to remind him of the important role that he plays in keeping Dr. King's dream alive!

A Man With a Dream

Martin Luther King Jr.

Dr. King dreamed that <u>all people would love each other and help each other</u>

1.

He also hoped that <u>people would not fight</u>

2.

I can keep his dream alive by <u>being nice to others and not fighting</u>.

3.

Learning about Dr. King has taught me <u>that it is good to have a dream. He also taught me that being mean is dumb</u>

4.

Timely Prompts

Pay tribute to Martin Luther King Jr. with thought-provoking prompts. Familiarize the class with Dr. King's role in history and how his memory is honored each January. Then ask each student to respond to one of the prompts below on provided paper. If desired, instruct each youngster to staple his completed writing inside a 9" x 12" construction paper folder. Then have him use a copy of the pattern on page 15, a length of yarn, and several construction paper leaves to embellish his folder as shown.

- Martin Luther King Jr. believed in solving disagreements without violence. Write about a time you solved a disagreement in a peaceful way.
- How might things be different in your school and neighborhood if Dr. King had not worked to change unfair laws?
- Dr. King once said, "Let freedom ring." What do you think he meant?

Stride Toward Freedom

Dr. Martin Luther King Jr. made great strides toward promoting freedom, peace, and understanding among all people. Highlight his accomplishments with a student-made display. Back a bulletin board with white paper and the title "Stride Toward Freedom" (which is also the title of Dr. King's first book). Make a class supply of the footprint pattern on page 16. After students have had a chance to study Dr. King's life, have each child complete a pattern, cut it out, and glue it on a sheet of construction paper. Then have him trim around the pattern to leave a ¼-inch border of color. Mount the projects on the board, along with a picture of Dr. King or a student-written timeline of his life.

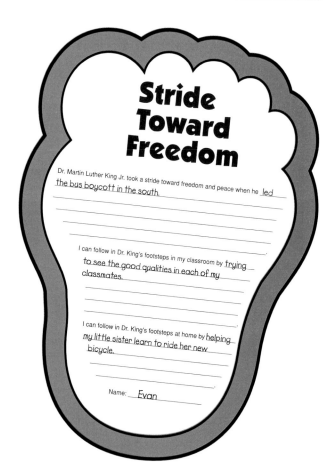

Stride Toward Freedom

Dr. Martin Luther King Jr. took a stride toward freedom and peace when he led the bus boycott in the south.

I can follow in Dr. King's footsteps in my classroom by trying to see the good qualities in each of my classmates.

I can follow in Dr. King's footsteps at home by helping my little sister learn to ride her new bicycle.

Name: Evan

Give Peace a Chance

Honor the contributions of Dr. Martin Luther King Jr. with a thought-provoking paragraph-writing activity. Share with students that Dr. King once stated, "Sooner or later all the people of the world will have to discover a way to live together in peace...." Discuss this remark and Dr. King's belief in nonviolent, peaceful forms of protest. Then give each student a nine-inch pastel paper circle and a crayon or marker. Have the student draw a peace symbol on the circle as shown. Then have him write a title in the left portion of the circle. In the right portion, have him write a short paragraph that describes how he can promote peace in his family, classroom, or neighborhood. Post the completed symbols on a bulletin board that's decorated with a large copy of Dr. King's quote.

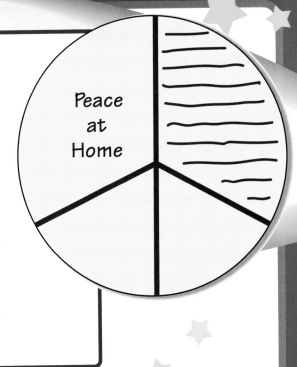

In remembrance of Martin Luther King, Jr.'s dream of peace and compassion for all, ask students to ponder their dreams for their community. Have each child write his thoughts on white paper and then trim the paper to create one large thought bubble and several small connecting bubbles. Provide the supplies that students need to create self-portraits like the ones shown; then mount each child's project for all to see.

adapted from an idea by Debbie Dalton, C. M. Bradley Elementary School, Warrenton, VA

Martin Luther King Jr. Project Patterns

Use with "Keeping the Dream Alive" on page 11.

TEC61174

A	Man	With	a	Dream
Martin		Luther		King Jr.

1.

Dr. King dreamed that _____

2.

He also hoped that _____

3.

I can keep his dream alive by _____

4.

Learning about Dr. King has taught me _____

TEC61174

Footprint Pattern
Use with "Stride Toward Freedom" on page 12.

Stride Toward Freedom

Dr. Martin Luther King Jr. took a stride toward freedom and peace when he _____

_____

_____

_____

_____

_____ .

I can follow in Dr. King's footsteps in my classroom by _____

_____

_____

_____

_____

_____ .

I can follow in Dr. King's footsteps at home by _____

_____

_____

_____

_____ .

Name: _____

TEC61174

Name _____

Dr. King's Dream

Read the passage.

Dr. King dreamed that all people would be treated fairly. He lived in a time when some laws were not fair. One law said that black children could not go to the same school as white children. Another law said that black people must sit at the back of city buses. Dr. King worked to change those laws.

He didn't try to change the laws by hurting people. Dr. King was a peaceful man. He tried peaceful ideas. He and other black people decided not to ride the buses at all. This is called a boycott. The people who ran the buses were mad. When no one rode the bus, they lost money! Dr. King and his friends did not give up. They won! The law was changed.

Dr. King led many marches. He gave speeches. He worked hard to make his dreams come true.

Circle the correct answer.

1. Dr. King wanted all people to be treated ___.	fairly	differently
2. Dr. King fought to change ___.	months	laws
3. Dr. King fought laws using ___ ways.	violent	peaceful
4. People decided to ___ the buses.	boycott	war
5. The bus owners lost ___.	tickets	money
6. Dr. King led ___.	lessons	marches
7. Dr. King gave ___.	speeches	papers
8. Dr. King worked ___.	hard	soon

Martin Luther King Jr.

Read the topic sentences and the supporting details below.
In front of each detail, circle the letter for the correct topic sentence.

Topic Sentences
A. Martin Luther King Jr. grew up in Atlanta, Georgia.
B. During his life, Martin had many personal accomplishments.
C. Martin was a civil rights leader.

Supporting Details

A B C 1. He was born on January 15, 1929.

A B C 2. He served as president of the group that ran the bus boycott in Montgomery, Alabama, in 1955.

A B C 3. He wrote five books.

A B C 4. He helped to organize the March on Washington in 1963.

A B C 5. His father was a minister, and his mother was a teacher.

A B C 6. He had one sister and one brother.

A B C 7. He won the Nobel Peace Prize in 1964.

A B C 8. He helped begin a major civil rights campaign in Chicago in 1966.

A B C 9. He was ordained as a minister in 1948.

Bonus Box: Choose one topic sentence from above. Use the topic sentence and its supporting details to write a paragraph about Martin Luther King Jr. Write the paragraph on the back of this sheet.

Remembering Martin Luther King Jr.

Cut out the sentences.
Read the sentences and arrange them in order.
Glue each sentence in place.

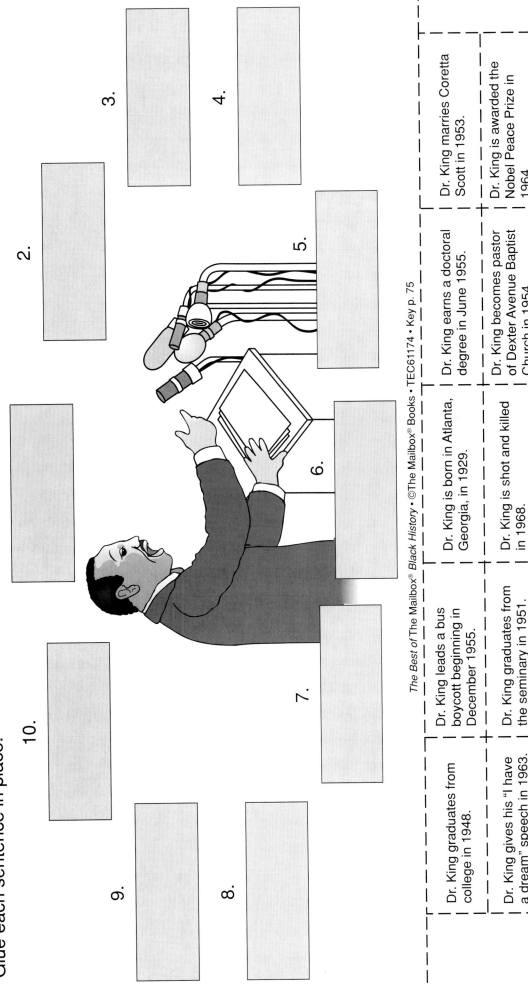

1.

2.

3.

4.

5.

6.

7.

8.

9.

10.

The Best of The Mailbox® *Black History* • ©The Mailbox® Books • TEC61174 • Key p. 75

Dr. King leads a bus boycott beginning in December 1955.	Dr. King is born in Atlanta, Georgia, in 1929.	Dr. King earns a doctoral degree in June 1955.	Dr. King marries Coretta Scott in 1953.
Dr. King graduates from the seminary in 1951.	Dr. King is shot and killed in 1968.	Dr. King becomes pastor of Dexter Avenue Baptist Church in 1954.	Dr. King is awarded the Nobel Peace Prize in 1964.
Dr. King graduates from college in 1948.			
Dr. King gives his "I have a dream" speech in 1963.			

19

Dr. King's Dream

Read the passage.
Answer the questions.

Years ago, black people and white people did not have the same rights. They had different schools and bathrooms. If a black person rode a bus, he had to give his seat to a white person. Martin Luther King Jr. felt that these things were wrong. He thought all people were equal. He wanted all people to be treated the same.

Dr. King tried to change things. He wrote speeches. He went to one town and helped people start a bus boycott. Black people stopped riding buses until they could sit in the same seats as white people. A few years later Dr. King led a peaceful march. He made a famous speech called "I have a dream."

Dr. King kept working to make sure that blacks and whites were treated fairly. He was killed in 1968. Each year on his birthday, we honor him because he solved problems in a peaceful way.

1. What was Dr. King's dream? _____

_____

2. Name two ways black people and white people weren't treated the same. _____

_____

_____

3. Why do we celebrate Dr. King's birthday? _____

_____

4. How do you think Dr. King solved problems peacefully? _____

_____

5. Circle the letter of the best title for this passage.
   A. How to Treat People   B. A Famous Person
   C. Dr. King and His Dream   D. Being the Same

Is That a Fact?

Read each statement below. Write "F" if the statement is a fact.
Write "O" if the statement is an opinion.

_____ 1. It is hard to picture what life was like when Martin Luther King Jr. was young.

_____ 2. Black Americans were not allowed to hold certain jobs.

_____ 3. King worked harder than anyone else for the civil rights movement.

_____ 4. He led the Montgomery bus boycott.

_____ 5. King made 208 speeches in just one year.

_____ 6. People liked King's "Letter From Birmingham Jail" more than anything else he wrote.

_____ 7. He asked people to help end segregation.

_____ 8. King's most important meeting about civil rights was with the president.

_____ 9. King's "I have a dream" speech was his best speech ever.

_____ 10. King was given the Nobel Peace Prize in 1964.

Bonus Box: For each opinion above, circle the words that helped you decide the statement was not a fact.

A Man to Remember

Circle the correct verb to complete each sentence. Then write the verb
in the blank.

1. Martin Luther King Jr. _____ battles with words rather
   than weapons.

   N. fighted   M. fought

2. When he was born, his parents _____ in Atlanta, Georgia.

   H. lived   B. live

3. He _____ to college when he was 15.

   E. goed   T. went

4. Martin _____ a boycott against the Montgomery bus
   system in 1955.

   N. led   R. leaded

5. The bus system _____ its unfair policies after a
   Supreme Court decision.

   D. changed   S. change

6. In 1963, Martin Luther King Jr. _____ his "I have a dream"
   speech in Washington, DC.

   T. gived   A. gave

7. Thousands of people _____ to Washington to hear this
   famous speech.

   I. came   N. come

8. Martin _____ the Nobel Peace Prize for his work with
   civil rights.

   A. won   G. winned

9. In 1983 Congress _____ the third Monday in January
   Martin Luther King Jr. Day.

   O. maked   A. made

10. Martin Luther King Jr. _____ a man whose work will
    be remembered.

    P. were   G. was

Who inspired Martin Luther King Jr. to change laws with peaceful methods?
To find out, write each circled letter above in its matching numbered blank below.

____ ____ ____ ____ ____ ____ ____   ____ ____ ____ ____ ____ ____
 1   8   2   9   3   1   8   10   6   4   5   2   7

The Best of The Mailbox® *Black History* • ©The Mailbox® Books • TEC61174 • Key p. 75

Quote This

Dr. Martin Luther King Jr. was an important voice in the fight for civil rights. His words are still quoted by others today. Use editor's symbols to add capital letters (a̲), commas (⌄), and quotation marks ("⌄ ⌄") to the quotes below.

1. my mother said I was as good as anyone Dr. King told a friend.	2. Dr. King said everyone can be great.	3. Dr. King told his followers if pushed, do not push back. if struck, do not strike back.
4. hate cannot drive out hate he stated. only love can do that.	5. Dr. King said love builds up and unites; hate tears down and destroys.	6. I can't be silent Dr. King explained. I am a citizen of the world.
7. sooner or later, all the people of the world will have to discover a way to live together he declared.	8. Dr. King said love is the key to the problems of the world.	9. This is our hope he told the crowd.
10. He stated we cannot walk alone.	11. we cannot turn back Dr. King advised.	12. Dr. King declared I have a dream today!

King's Computations

Dr. Martin Luther King Jr. was born on January 15, 1929. He is best remembered as a promoter of peace and equality for all people. He was assassinated on April 4, 1968. Several years later his birthday was declared a federal holiday.

To find out what year King's birthday was made a federal holiday, work through the problems below. Write the answer to the first problem on the blank provided. Then use that answer in the first blank of the second problem. Use the answer to the second problem in the first blank of the third problem. Continue in this manner through problem 14.

1. Subtract the year of King's birth from the year of his death to learn his age when he died.

    _____ – _____ = _____

2. Multiply by the number of the day of the month on which he was born.

    _____ x _____ = _____

3. Divide by 5.

    _____ ÷ _____ = _____

4. Reverse the order of the digits.

    _____

5. Multiply by the number of months in a year.

    _____ x _____ = _____

6. Divide by the number of the day of the month on which King died.

    _____ ÷ _____ = _____

7. Subtract the last two digits of the year in which King was born.

    _____ – _____ = _____

8. Divide by the number of letters in his last name.

    _____ ÷ _____ = _____

9. Double this number.

    _____ x _____ = _____

10. Subtract 136 from this number.

    _____ – _____ = _____

11. Add the number of days in January.

    _____ + _____ = _____

12. Double this number.

    _____ x _____ = _____

13. Switch the second and third digits.

    _____

14. Subtract 1.

    _____ – _____ = _____

The year that Martin Luther King Jr.'s birthday became a national holiday was _____.

Martin's Mission

Martin Luther King Jr.'s goal was to change the world in a peaceful manner. He organized marches and wrote letters. He also gave speeches to try to change people's minds about racial equality. A quotation from Dr. King is hidden in the chart below. Follow the directions to uncover the quote.

Directions: Compare the two fractions in each box. If they are equivalent, shade the box lightly with your pencil. If the fractions are not equivalent, cross out the box by drawing a large X through it.

$\frac{1}{2}$ $\frac{2}{4}$	$\frac{3}{5}$ $\frac{2}{3}$	$\frac{1}{4}$ $\frac{3}{12}$	$\frac{12}{30}$ $\frac{2}{5}$	$\frac{9}{10}$ $\frac{16}{20}$
powerful	everyone	in	without	Remember
$\frac{1}{6}$ $\frac{5}{30}$	$\frac{6}{8}$ $\frac{3}{4}$	$\frac{4}{16}$ $\frac{8}{32}$	$\frac{24}{32}$ $\frac{2}{4}$	$\frac{1}{7}$ $\frac{2}{14}$
and	It is	history,	freedom	sword
$\frac{2}{3}$ $\frac{5}{18}$	$\frac{3}{2}$ $1\frac{1}{2}$	$\frac{3}{8}$ $\frac{10}{24}$	$\frac{15}{21}$ $\frac{5}{7}$	$\frac{6}{4}$ $1\frac{1}{4}$
together	a	when	wounding....	children
$\frac{3}{10}$ $\frac{6}{20}$	$\frac{8}{10}$ $\frac{4}{5}$	$\frac{14}{28}$ $\frac{3}{7}$	$\frac{18}{32}$ $\frac{9}{16}$	$\frac{6}{36}$ $\frac{1}{6}$
just	weapon	reaches	It is	that
$\frac{4}{3}$ $1\frac{1}{3}$	$\frac{5}{25}$ $\frac{2}{5}$	$\frac{9}{12}$ $\frac{3}{4}$	$\frac{2}{6}$ $\frac{3}{18}$	$\frac{18}{2}$ 9
weapon.	peace	which	marches	heals.
$\frac{31}{5}$ $6\frac{1}{6}$	$\frac{10}{4}$ $2\frac{1}{2}$	$\frac{1}{11}$ $\frac{3}{33}$	$\frac{8}{64}$ $\frac{1}{8}$	$\frac{72}{10}$ $7\frac{2}{5}$
equal.	unique	cuts	a	always.

Now complete the following quotation by writing on the lines below the words from the shaded boxes. Begin with the first column on the left. List the words in order from top to bottom. Then move to the second column, and so on.

"Nonviolence is a _____

_____

_____."

Martin Luther King Jr.
Why We Can't Wait (1964)

I Have a Dream

Divide to answer each question about Martin Luther King Jr.

O. When was he born? $3858 \div 2 =$ _____

F. At what age did he go to college? $165 \div 11 =$ _____

H. When did he marry Coretta Scott? $7812 \div 4 =$ _____

T. When did he publish his first book? $7832 \div 4 =$ _____

E. How many books did he write? $410 \div 82 =$ _____

N. In what year did he give his "I have a dream" speech? $5889 \div 3 =$ _____

A. In what year did he win the Nobel Peace Prize? $3928 \div 2 =$ _____

C. At what age did he die? $975 \div 25 =$ _____

I. In what year was he shot? $3936 \div 2 =$ _____

R. In what year was Martin Luther King Jr. Day first observed? $5958 \div 3 =$ _____

What did Martin Luther King Jr. want his children to be known for?
To answer this question, write the letters above on the matching numbered lines below.

___ ___ ___   ___ ___ ___ ___ ___ ___ ___   ___ ___   ___ ___ ___ ___ ___
1958 1953 5   39 1929 1963 1958 5 1963 1958   1929 15   1958 1953 5 1968 1986

___ ___ ___ ___ ___ ___ ___ ___ ___
39 1953 1964 1986 1964 39 1958 5 1986

What If…?

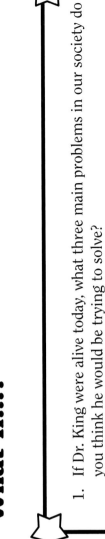

I have a *dream.*

What if Martin Luther King Jr. were alive today? You probably know lots about Dr. King. He was a black civil rights leader who was born in 1929 and died in 1968. He was only 39 years old when he died. His birthday is celebrated each year as a tribute to his ideas on equal rights and nonviolence.

A lot has changed since the days of King's peaceful protests, but the world still needs equality and peace. Think about how Martin Luther King Jr. might affect our society if he were alive today. Read the questions on the right. Choose three to answer in short paragraphs. Write your paragraphs on another sheet of paper.

1. If Dr. King were alive today, what three main problems in our society do you think he would be trying to solve?

2. If he were alive today, do you think Dr. King would be holding a political office? If so, which one? If not, why not?

3. Which groups of people would Dr. King most likely be helping with equal rights today?

4. In his lifetime, Dr. King received many honorary university degrees. He was also chosen as *Time* magazine's Man of the Year for 1963. He won the Nobel Peace Prize in 1964. Dr. King was a minister, a speaker, and a respected civil rights leader. If he were teaching in a university today, what subjects do you think he might be teaching? Why?

5. If Dr. King were alive today, he would be happy with the progress made in some civil rights areas. Finish this paragraph starter, spoken by Dr. King: "I am so glad that…"

6. If Martin Luther King Jr. were alive today, do you think we would be celebrating his birthday this year? Why or why not?

Through the Years

Read the following passage about Dr. Martin Luther King Jr. Then fill in each blank on the timeline with a date and fact from the passage. Use the boldfaced dates in the passage to help you.

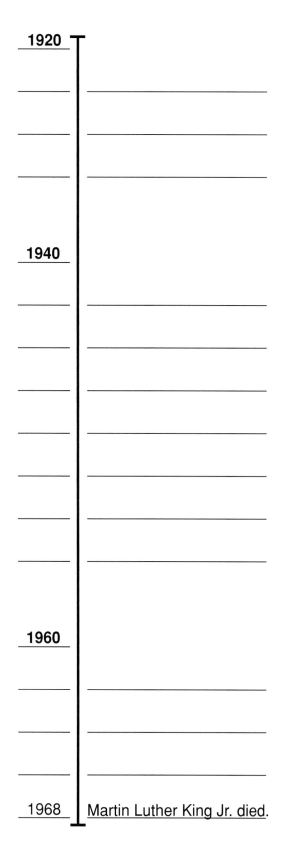

1920

1940

1960

1968 | Martin Luther King Jr. died.

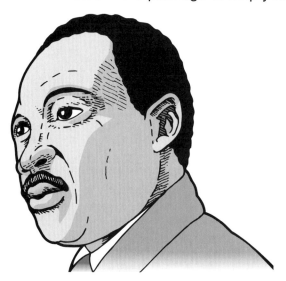

Martin Luther King Jr. was born January 15, **1929.** Martin grew up in Atlanta, Georgia, in the **1930s.** In **1935,** he started school. But he could not go to school with his white friends. Martin had to go to a school for black children. He was told his white friends could not play with him anymore.

By the time Martin was 15, he had finished high school and was starting college. He earned his first college degree in **1948.** Martin earned his second college degree in **1951.** Then he moved to Boston to earn a Ph.D. It was in Boston that Martin met Coretta Scott. Martin and Coretta were married in **1953.**

In **1954,** they moved to Montgomery, Alabama. Martin became a pastor there. He helped set up a boycott of public buses in **1955.** Black people were protesting a law that said they had to ride at the backs of the buses. Black people refused to ride the public buses until the law was changed. In **1956,** the law was changed. Martin became well known for helping southern black people peacefully stand up for their rights.

In **1957,** Martin and a group of pastors founded the Southern Christian Leadership Conference. They worked together to help black people stand up for their rights. Martin met with President John F. Kennedy in **1962** to talk about civil rights.

Martin gave his famous speech, "I have a dream," on August 28, **1963.** Martin Luther King Jr. received the Nobel Peace Prize in **1964.** No one as young as Martin had ever won the award before.

Enrich your celebration of Black History
Month with the following kid-pleasing ideas.

Famous Firsts Lotto

Pique your students' interest in Black American firsts! Give each child a copy of page 32 and the picture cards from page 33. She also needs a quart-size resealable plastic bag for game storage. To prepare her gameboard, the child cuts out the cards and gameboard on page 32. She randomly glues the cards on the gameboard spaces. Then she cuts out the picture cards. As students work, cut out a set of picture cards and place them in a container.

To play, announce a type of game such as "Three (four) in a row" or "Four corners." Next, draw a picture card from your container and read the person's name aloud. The student finds her copy of the card and places it on her gameboard atop the person's famous first. Ask a volunteer to identify the corresponding famous first. Then have each child check the accuracy of her card placement and make any needed adjustment. Place your card in a discard pile and draw another card from the container. Continue play as described.

The first student to cover a winning set of game spaces exclaims "Famous firsts!" Visually confirm her win and then have her read aloud the matches. If desired, have the winner of the first game become the caller for the second game and so on until game time is over. Then have students store their games for play on another day. Before long your scholars will know these famous firsts by heart and they'll be ready to track down 12 more for a second edition of the game!

Colleen Majors, Stephen Girard School, Philadelphia, PA

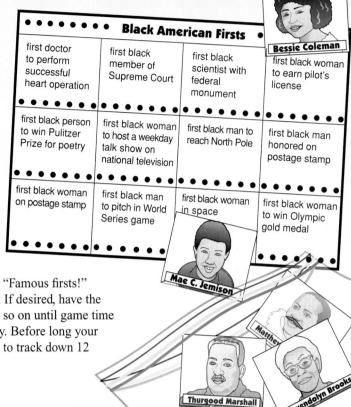

Black American Firsts

first doctor to perform successful heart operation	first black member of Supreme Court	first black scientist with federal monument	
first black person to win Pulitzer Prize for poetry	first black woman to host a weekday talk show on national television	first black man to reach North Pole	first black man honored on postage stamp
first black woman on postage stamp	first black man to pitch in World Series game	first black woman in space	first black woman to win Olympic gold medal

Bessie Coleman — first black woman to earn pilot's license

Mae C. Jemison

Thurgood Marshall · Mathew · Gwendolyn Brooks

All-Star Boxes

Here's a perfect project for rookie researchers! Collect a class supply of empty cube-shaped tissue boxes and then cut blank white paper to fit the sides and tops of the boxes. Also display an assortment of children's books that contain biographical information about Black American achievers. After students have investigated the books you've gathered, ask each child to complete a copy of "Black American Achiever" from page 33. To do this, he names the Black American achiever he will research. Then he finds four interesting facts about the person, copies each fact on his paper, and writes where the facts were found.

When his research is approved for publication (by you), he copies each fact on a piece of precut paper. Then he decorates the papers and glues them to the sides of a tissue box. On another piece of precut paper he illustrates and labels the Black American he researched. He glues this paper to the top of his box. After each child shares his report with the class, exhibit the all-star boxes for further investigation.

Colleen Dabney, Williamsburg, VA

Aretha Franklin

Fact 1
Aretha started her singing career when she was 12 years old.

Fact 2
She is called the Queen of Soul.

Poetic Tributes

During Black History Month, honor famous Americans with this poetry-writing activity. Use grade-appropriate resources to familiarize students with the achievements of chosen Black Americans. To pay tribute to the featured people, give each youngster a copy of page 34. The student identifies a chosen Black American as his poetry topic. Then he follows the activity directions to draft a poem about the person. After he edits his poem, he writes a final draft on a half sheet of writing paper, mounts it onto a sheet of construction paper, and then decorates his work as desired.

Traci A. Guth, McPherson Elementary School, Chicago, IL

Thurgood Marshall

judge
proud, first
studied, graduated, helped
worked for equal rights
hero

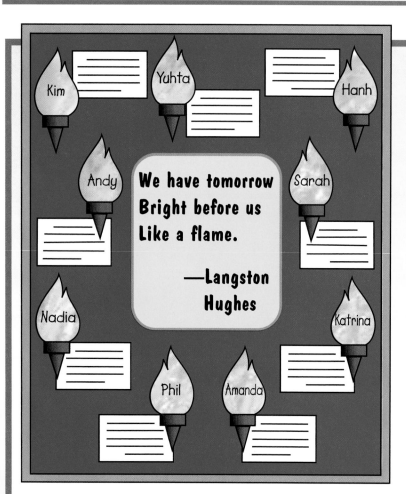

Spotlight Black History Month with the help of a famous Black American poet. Have each student cut out a flame shape from white construction paper. After coloring the flame with yellow and orange chalk, the student smudges the colors with a tissue and uses a black marker to label the flame with his name. Then he glues a small black rectangle and triangle to the flame as shown. Post the flames with the lines from Langston Hughes's poem "Youth" as shown. Finally, have each student add to the display a paragraph describing the bright future he is planning for himself.

Andrea Troisi, LaSalle Middle School
Niagara Falls, NY

Black History Month Activity Cards

Celebrate Black History Month with the ready-to-use activity cards featured on pages 35–38. Glue a copy of the cards onto posterboard and then laminate the poster board and cut apart the cards. Store the cards in a box, or punch a hole in the corner of each card and store on a metal ring. Display your students' finished work from the cards on a bulletin board titled "They Believed. They Achieved!"

PIECING TOGETHER
AFRICAN AMERICAN
HISTORY

GEORGE WASHINGTON CARVER	COLIN POWELL	MALCOLM X
MARIAN ANDERSON	CARL LEWIS	WILMA RUDOLPH
ARTHUR ASHE	ROSA PARKS	MARTIN LUTHER KING

Piece together facts about famous African Americans during Black History Month with this eye-catching display. Make a class supply of the pattern on page 39. Have each student write the name of a famous African American in the center square; then have him color the rest of the pattern. Mount the patterns to make a giant quilt. Choose one square from the quilt each morning during February; then have the student who researched that famous figure share facts about him or her.

Colleen Dabney
Williamsburg Christian Academy
Williamsburg, VA

first doctor to perform successful heart operation	first black woman in space	first black member of Supreme Court	first black woman to host a weekday talk show on national television
first black woman on postage stamp	first black man to reach North Pole	first black man to pitch in World Series game	first black person to win Pulitzer Prize for poetry
first black woman to win Olympic gold medal	first black man honored on postage stamp	first black scientist with federal monument	first black woman to earn pilot's license

Note to the teacher: Use with "Famous Firsts Lotto" on page 29.

Matthew Henson	**Alice Coachman**	**Booker T. Washington**	**Oprah Winfrey**
Mae C. Jemison	**Thurgood Marshall**	**Bessie Coleman**	**Daniel Hale Williams**
Satchel Paige	**Gwendolyn Brooks**	**George Washington Carver**	**Harriet Tubman**

Black American Achiever Form
Use with "All-Star Boxes" on page 29.

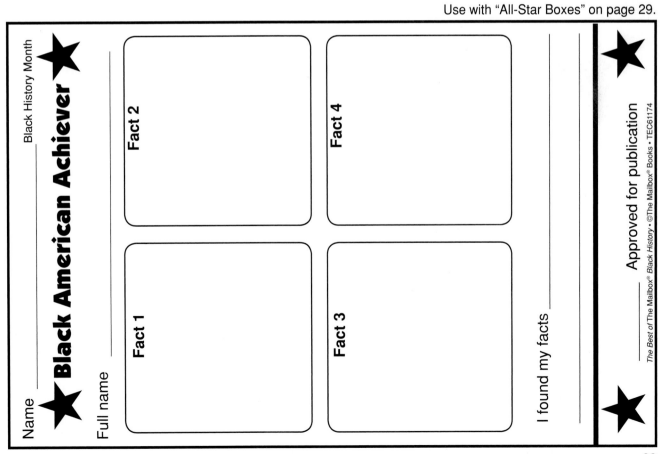

Black History Month

Black American Achiever

Name _____

Full name _____

Fact 1

Fact 2

Fact 3

Fact 4

I found my facts _____

Approved for publication

The Best of The Mailbox® Black History • ©The Mailbox® Books • TEC61174

Poetry Planner

Write your topic on the line below.
List words that tell about your topic in the correct columns.

Topic: _____

Nouns	Adjectives	Verbs

Now use words from the chart to write a poem below.

_____
(noun)

_____, _____
(adjective)   (adjective)

_____, _____, _____
(verb)   (verb)   (verb)

_____
(four-word phrase)

_____
(noun)

2.

Mary McLeod Bethune (1875–1955) worked to improve educational opportunities for blacks. Because there were no schools for black children in her hometown, Mary didn't start school until she was 11 years old. After college, she became a teacher. She opened a school for black girls in Florida. The school became Bethune-Cookman College. Mary later worked in the United States government to help end racial discrimination.

To Do: Mary McLeod Bethune believed that education would help black people fight discrimination. How do you think your education will help you 20 years from now? Write your answer in paragraph form.

TEC61174

4.

Shirley Chisholm (1924–2005) was the first black woman to serve in the United States Congress. Chisholm was a member of the House of Representatives from 1969–1983. She worked hard to serve the people that she represented in New York. She also worked to make sure our country's laws met the needs of more people.

To Do: Shirley Chisholm's parents advised her: "Keep your head high. Always give the best you have within you to give. Somebody will recognize it in the future." Do you agree or disagree? Write your answer.

TEC61174

1.

Langston Hughes (1902–1967) was a writer and poet. He wrote about the inequality suffered by blacks in America. He also wrote plays and humorous stories about black life. These stories were known as the Simple stories because the main character was a wise man nicknamed "Simple."

To Do: Langston Hughes wrote many poems about the lives and problems of black people. Write a poem about your own life and some of the problems you face.

TEC61174

3.

Frederick Douglass (1818–1895) lived a hard life as a slave in the South. Eventually he escaped to the North and freedom. At the age of 24 he made his first speech against slavery. He also founded a newspaper. He was devoted to ending slavery and fighting for black rights. Douglass also helped recruit blacks for the Union Army during the Civil War.

To Do: Frederick Douglass fought hard to end slavery in America. What injustice or problem would you like to see come to an end? Divide a piece of paper in half. On one half, illustrate the problem. On the other half, illustrate a possible solution.

TEC61174

Note to the teacher: Use with "Black History Month Activity Cards" on page 31.

6.

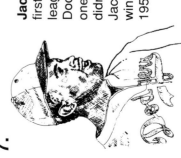

Bill Cosby (1937–) is a comedian and was the star of his own program, "The Cosby Show." He costarred in the mid-'60s in the action series "I Spy." He also created and hosted the "Fat Albert and the Cosby Kids" cartoon. Cosby has sold more comedy recordings than anyone in the world. He's also the author of several popular books.

To Do: Bill Cosby played the father of five children on "The Cosby Show." He also has several children of his own. List at least five things you think fathers should know about raising kids.

TEC61174

8.

Sojourner Truth (1797?–1883) was the first black woman to make speeches against slavery. She worked to improve life for blacks living in Washington, DC. She also helped to find jobs and homes in the city for escaped slaves.

To Do: You are preparing to make a speech about a problem that is very important to you. Someone has warned you that there may be some people in the audience who disagree with you. Will you still make your speech? Why or why not? Write your answer.

TEC61174

5.

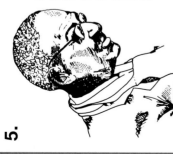

George Washington Carver (1864–1943) was a great scientist. He believed that he could help the poor in the South by teaching them about farming. He made more than 300 products from the peanut plant, including face powder, ink, and soap. He also worked to improve understanding between blacks and whites.

To Do: In 1939, Carver received a medal for his contributions to science. Design a medal to give to George Washington Carver.

TEC61174

7.

Jackie Robinson (1919–1972) was the first black player to play American major league baseball. He played for the Brooklyn Dodgers in 1947. His first year was a hard one. Many people believed a black man didn't belong in the major leagues. But Jackie didn't give up. He helped the Dodgers win six National League pennants and the 1955 World Series.

To Do: Jackie Robinson helped to make it possible for other black players to play in the major leagues. Design a certificate honoring Jackie for his contributions to sports and civil rights.

TEC61174

36

Note to the teacher: Use with "Black History Month Activity Cards" on page 31.

10.

Thurgood Marshall (1908–1993) became the first black ever appointed to serve on the United States Supreme Court. He started his career as a lawyer. Marshall worked to eliminate separate schools for blacks and whites.

TEC61174

To Do: Thurgood Marshall believed in protecting human rights. Write a paragraph explaining what you think the rights of schoolchildren are.

12.

Coretta Scott King (1927–2006) worked for the civil rights of blacks and other minorities. She was the widow of Dr. Martin Luther King, Jr. While her husband was working to win more rights for black Americans, Mrs. King gave speeches and lectures. After Dr. King was killed, Mrs. King continued working for civil rights.

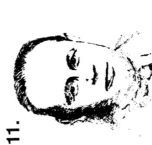

TEC61174

To Do: What rights do you think all Americans should enjoy? Make a list of at least ten of these rights.

9.

Matthew Henson (1866–1955) worked as the captain's cabin boy on a boat. He loved traveling. Later Matthew worked for Robert Peary, a naval engineer. When Peary decided to try to reach the North Pole, Matthew was hired to go with him. After several failures, they reached the North Pole. Matthew was chosen to plant the American flag in the frozen ground.

TEC61174

To Do: Matthew Henson was the first man to set foot on the North Pole. What would you like to be the first person to do? Write your answer.

11.

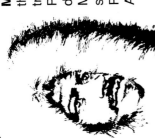

Charles Richard Drew (1904–1950) almost became a professional football player. But instead he decided to become a doctor. He is known for setting up some of the nation's first blood banks. His blood banks saved many lives, particularly during World War II.

TEC61174

To Do: Charles Drew once resigned from a job. The reason? He was told to collect and store blood donated by black people separately from the blood donated by whites. Write a letter to Charles Drew telling him what you think of his decision to resign.

The Best of The Mailbox® • *Black History* • ©The Mailbox® Books • TEC61174

Note to the teacher: Use with "Black History Month Activity Cards" on page 31.

37

13.

Althea Gibson (1927–2003) became one of the world's greatest tennis players. She was the first black to play at Wimbledon, England. She won many tennis titles. After she retired from tennis, she became a professional golfer.

To Do: Do some research about another famous black female athlete, Wilma Rudolph. How are she and Althea Gibson alike? How are they different? Write your answer.

TEC61174

14.

Jesse Jackson (1941–) is an American civil rights activist, political leader, and Baptist minister. In 1984 and 1988 he ran for the Democratic nomination for president. Even though he did not win either time, he focused attention on the problems of blacks and other minority groups in America. His work includes helping black students get a better education.

To Do: Pretend that Jesse Jackson has asked you to write a plan. The plan should convince kids like yourself to stay away from drugs and alcohol. Write your plan. Tell why you think it could work.

TEC61174

15.

Garrett Morgan (1877–1963) invented the first gas mask. It was called the Morgan Safety Hood. It saved many lives. He and his brother once used the masks to rescue 32 men from a tunnel explosion. Garrett also invented the first traffic-light signal.

To Do: Think of a problem (big or small) in the world today. Now think of an invention that might solve that problem. Draw a picture of your invention. Give it a name. Write a brief description of how your invention works.

TEC61174

16.

Paul Robeson (1898–1976) was an outstanding actor and singer. He was featured in many movies and on many record albums. Robeson performed in many famous plays. He also worked in the peace and civil rights movements of the late 1930s.

To Do: Paul Robeson was a man of many talents. He was a star athlete in college, a singer and an actor, a civil rights activist, and an author. Everyone has talents. Make a collage to illustrate some of your talents.

TEC61174

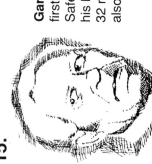

Note to the teacher: Use with "Black History Month Activity Cards" on page 31.

Quilt Square Pattern

Use with "Piecing Together African American History" on page 31.

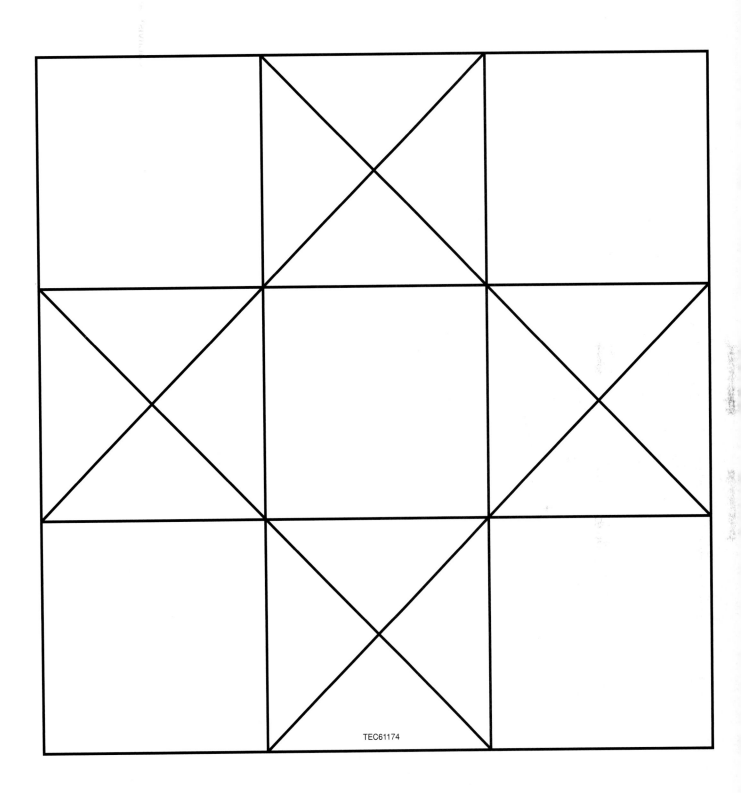

TEC61174

Making a Difference:
A Memory Game

Materials Needed for Each Student
white construction paper copy of the game cards
    below and on page 41
index card
crayons
scissors
resealable plastic bag

How to Use Pages 40 and 41
1. Remind students that February is Black History Month, a special time for recognizing the past and current achievements of Black Americans.
2. Ask students to follow along on their own cards as you read aloud the information about each African American featured. Supplement the information as desired.
3. Have each student personalize his index card and then color and cut out his game cards.
4. Instruct each student to store his game cards and personalized index card in his resealable plastic bag.
5. To play a Concentration-type game, pair students and share with them the provided playing instructions.

Playing Instructions for Each Student Pair
1. Shuffle one set of cards and arrange them facedown on a playing surface.
2. Determine which player will take his turn first.
3. The first player turns over two cards. If a picture card and its corresponding information card are revealed, the player identifies the African American shown and his or her achievement(s). Then he keeps the cards and turns over two more. If the two cards turned over do not match as described above, the player turns them facedown again, and his turn is over.
4. The second player takes his turn in a similar manner.
5. Play continues in this manner until all of the cards are matched or game time is over.
6. The child with the most cards wins the game.

Making a Difference Game Cards

I am Garrett Morgan.	I am Oprah Winfrey.	I am Louis Armstrong.
1877–1963 × TEC61174	1954– ◆ TEC61174	1901–1971 ◎ TEC61174
I was an inventor. One of my most famous inventions was the three-way traffic stoplight. TEC61174 ×	I am a talk-show host, an actress, and a TV producer. I was the first African American to own a major TV-and-film-production studio. TEC61174 ◆	I was a famous jazz musician. I played the cornet and trumpet. I also sang. TEC61174 ◎

   The Best of The Mailbox® *Black History* • ©The Mailbox® Books • TEC61174

I am **Guion Bluford, Jr.**  1942– TEC61174 ▲	I am **Jesse Owens.**  1913–1980 TEC61174 ■	I am **Maya Angelou.**  1928– TEC61174 :
I am an astronaut. I became the first African American to fly in space. I flew aboard the *Challenger* space shuttle. TEC61174 ▲	I was a track-and-field star. I set seven world records during my career. TEC61174 ■	I am a famous writer. I was chosen by President Bill Clinton to write and recite a poem for his presidential inauguration. TEC61174 :
I am **Rosa Parks.**  1913–2005 TEC61174 ●	I am **Marian Anderson.**  1897–1993 TEC61174 =	I am **Booker T. Washington.**  1856–1915 TEC61174 Z
I was a civil rights leader. I was arrested for refusing to give up my seat on a public bus. TEC61174 ●	I was a concert singer. I was the first African American soloist to sing with the Metropolitan Opera of New York City. TEC61174 =	I was a teacher. I started a school for African American students. The school was called Tuskegee Institute. TEC61174 Z

Artist Extraordinaire

Meet Romare Bearden
1912?–1988

Award-winning artist and North Carolina native Romare Bearden is best remembered for his collage-style artwork. His childhood years were spent in North Carolina, the Harlem district of New York City, and Pittsburgh. His family taught him to value his African American heritage and to appreciate the arts. After graduating from high school, he played professional baseball, served in the army, and worked as a social worker. He also wrote songs, painted, and studied philosophy. Bearden's hunger to express his personal and cultural identity as a Black American led him in search of art styles which allowed him this freedom. When he began experimenting with collage, Bearden found his voice and his artistic talents were widely recognized and applauded. His success with collage earned him numerous awards, including the National Medal of Arts in 1987. It also gave him an opportunity to promote the works of other Black Americans in his field—which, for Bearden, was perhaps most significant of all.

Examples of Bearden's Work

Ask your school's art teacher or librarian to assist you in finding books that feature collages by Bearden.

Liza

Creating Collages

Bearden's first collages, called *photomontages,* were made using cutouts from photographs. Tell students that Bearden's artwork focused on his life; then have each child choose an activity from his own life to feature in a collage. To make a collage, a student cuts photographs from discarded newspapers and magazines and glues them on a sheet of construction paper to his liking. For additional creativity, explain that Bearden's earlier works often featured cutouts that were out of proportion, for example an extra large face atop a tiny body. Encourage students to try this technique. Be sure to set aside time for students to share their creations with the class.

Painted Paper Collages

In his later collages, which he called *paintings,* Bearden cut his shapes from prepainted paper. To give students a hand at this collage form, set aside two days. On the first day have each child visualize a self-reflecting collage and paint pieces of white construction paper for use in her artwork. On the second day, have her cut desired shapes from her prepainted papers and glue them on a sheet of construction paper. Bearden found that listening to jazz while he worked gave his artwork a musical feel. Why not try this approach with your artists as well!

Leading the Way

Contemporary Black American Achievers

Celebrate Black history with this introduction to six Americans who are tops in their fields. The thought-provoking ideas are just what you need to share the inspiring stories and achievements of these present-day heroes!

☆ Meet the Achievers ☆

Use this clue-filled reproducible activity to familiarize students with the featured achievers. Give each student a copy of page 45. Read each set of clues aloud, and then have each youngster cut out the pictures. Have her place each picture by the appropriate set of clues, using her reasoning skills and any prior knowledge she has about the individuals to guide her decisions. After every student is satisfied with her work, confirm the correct pairings. Instruct students to glue the pictures in place and color each ribbon by the code.

Next, invite students to tell any additional facts they know about the featured people. Lead a class discussion to explore how these Americans and their accomplishments influence people's lives. Students are sure to agree that from protecting U.S. interests to being role models, these achievers make a difference!

☆ In Agreement ☆

Colin Powell and Condoleezza Rice have played key roles in recent U.S. history. As the secretary of state, Powell was instrumental in negotiating the release of American hostages in China. Rice, the first female national security adviser, helped establish an agreement between Russia and the United States to reduce nuclear weapons. She went on to become secretary of state. Share these and other desired examples to help students understand the influence of these leaders.

Next, tell students that they are negotiators too! Clarify that *negotiate* means "to discuss a problem in order to reach an agreement." Guide students to identify familiar situations in which negotiation skills are helpful, such as when two friends want to play different games or when two siblings want to ride in the front seat of their parents' car. Then give each child a copy of a form similar to the one shown. Ask him to use the provided format to summarize and illustrate a time he negotiated with someone. Then invite your young negotiators to share their examples with the class.

Problem	Discussion	Result
My parents didn't want me to stay up late.	I asked if I could stay up just a half hour later. They asked if I would promise to wake up on time.	I promised, and they said, "Okay."

☆ The Winner's Circle ☆

What does it take to reach the top? In many cases, it takes hard work and a winning attitude. To illustrate this point, share the provided information about Vonetta Flowers, Tiger Woods, and Denzel Washington. Discuss with students the obstacles that each person overcame and how his or her perseverance paid off. Suggest that having goals focused these heroes' efforts and contributed to their success. Invite students to tell the class about their goals. Then have each child label a provided trophy cutout with her name, a goal, and what she might do to accomplish her goal. Showcase students' completed trophies on a bulletin board titled "Winning Dreams for the Future."

Andrea
I want to be a veterinarian when I grow up. I can help at the animal shelter to learn about animals.

Vonetta Flowers: When Vonetta failed to qualify as an Olympic long jumper, she didn't give up her Olympic dream. Instead, she decided to try out for the bobsled team. She exercised early every morning before work to prepare. She was the first Black American to win a Winter Olympic Games gold medal.

Tiger Woods: When Tiger first started playing golf, there were not many black players. That did not stop Tiger, though. He loved to golf and wanted to become the best. He practiced faithfully and became the first golf player of African or Asian heritage to win a major championship.

Denzel Washington: Early in Denzel's acting career, he struggled to find work and had very little money. With his wife's encouragement, he continued to pursue acting jobs. After many years of hard work, he became the second Black American to win an Academy Award for best actor.

puzzles
baking things
soccer
cooking
singing
Sammy
I can help my dad cook meals for my neighb...

☆ Gifted Hands ☆

Help your students realize that everyone can make a difference! Tell students that when Benjamin Carson was a young boy, he didn't do well in school. That is, until his mother convinced him that he could do better and sparked his interest in reading. Years later, he became a world-famous surgeon. Explain that some people say Dr. Carson has gifted hands because he has successfully operated on many very ill children when other doctors did not think it was possible. Point out that Dr. Carson believes in developing one's gifts. He encourages people to find out what they do well and then put those talents to good use.

To celebrate your students' talents, help them brainstorm things they are good at. Then give each youngster a light-colored hand cutout. On one side, he labels the fingers with his talents and signs his name on the palm. On the other side, he writes a good use for a chosen talent. What a handy reminder of students' special gifts!

Name _____

All-Star Achievers

Cut out the pictures.
Follow your teacher's directions to match the people with the clues.
Then, for each person, choose the best word from the code. Color the ribbon.

Use with "Meet the Achievers" on page 43.

Contemporary Black Americans
Identifying famous Americans

Color Code
sports = red
medicine = blue
government = green
entertainment = yellow

A
- Was a track star
- Coached by her husband
- Won an Olympic Games gold medal for bobsledding

B
- Won many military awards
- Retired four-star army general
- Advised the president about what was happening in other countries

C
- Learned to enjoy reading
- Sometimes called "Miracle Hands"
- Famous surgeon

D
- Plays the piano
- Speaks Russian
- Gives advice to the president

E
- Played football in high school
- Studied acting
- Won an Academy Award for best actor

F
- Was named Eldrick
- Started playing golf before he was three years old
- Youngest player to win the Masters Golf Tournament

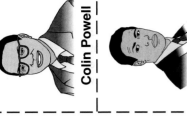
Colin Powell

Denzel Washington

Condoleezza Rice

Tiger Woods

Benjamin Carson

Vonetta Flowers

The Best of The Mailbox® *Black History* • ©The Mailbox® Books • TEC61174 • Key p. 76

Black History Month
by the Numbers

This clue-filled math activity leads to countless facts about famous Black Americans! And what better time to uncover this information than Black History Month? Each day of your study, post a different math problem that has an answer related to a significant fact in black history (refer to "Notable Numbers" below). Provide time for students to solve the problem. At the end of the day, invite volunteers to share their solutions. After verifying the answer, explain the significance of this number in relation to Black History Month. If desired, enlist students' help to find additional number-related facts about famous Black Americans and create corresponding math problems.

adapted from an idea by Laura Covell
St. Joseph Child Development Center, Kansas City, MO

Harriet Tubman

Mary McLeod Bethune

Matthew Henson

Notable Numbers

1: On December 1, 1955, Rosa Parks refused to give up her seat on a public bus. As a result, Parks became a key figure in the Civil Rights movement.

6: On April 6, 1909, Matthew Henson was the first Black American to reach the North Pole. Henson accompanied Robert Peary on the expedition to this site.

8: Mae Carol Jemison orbited the earth in the space shuttle *Endeavour* for 8 days. She was the first Black American woman in outer space.

11: Mary McLeod Bethune was 11 years old before a school was opened near her home and she was able to attend. As an adult, she dedicated her life to the education of blacks and created Bethune-Cookman College.

15: Martin Luther King Jr. was only 15 years old when he entered college. He worked hard to end segregation and promote peace.

17: Duke Ellington was 17 years old when he wrote his first song. He became a great jazz composer who has had a lasting influence on the field of music.

23: June 23 is Wilma Rudolph Day in Tennessee. After overcoming physical disabilities, Wilma Rudolph won three gold medals in the 1960 Olympics track-and-field events.

24: Thurgood Marshall served as a Supreme Court justice for 24 years. He was the first Black American on the U.S. Supreme Court.

26: Rebecca Lee Crumpler was 26 years old when she entered medical school. She became the first Black American woman to become a doctor.

44: Hank Aaron's baseball uniform number was 44. Aaron hit 755 home runs during his career in the major leagues.

100: Basketball player Wilt Chamberlain was the first player to score 100 points in one NBA game. Chamberlain was named the NBA's Player of the Decade for 1957–1966.

300: Harriet Tubman took 300 slaves to freedom using the Underground Railroad. Many years later, a postage stamp was designed in her honor, making her the first Black American woman to have her picture on a stamp.

See pages 47–49 for math reproducibles.

Making a Difference

Inventions created by Black Americans are all around us. Many have become important parts of our daily lives. Learn about some Black American inventors' contributions to society. Use the ordered pairs on the grid below to fill in each blank.

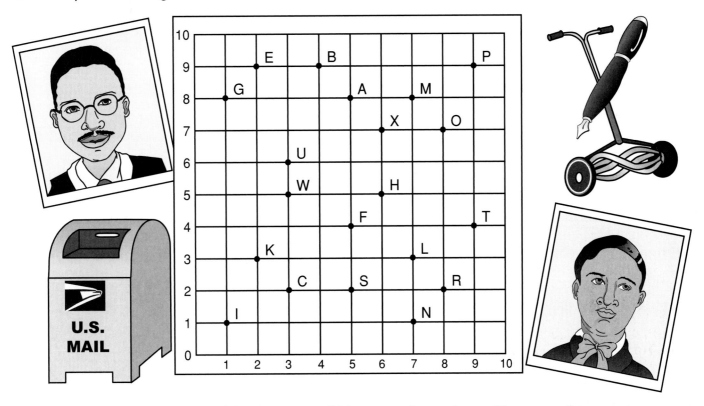

Lonnie Johnson was working on one of his many inventions. He wanted to create

a ___ ___ ___ ___   ___ ___ ___ ___ that didn't harm the environment. Suddenly, a
   (6,5) (2,9) (5,8) (9,4)   (9,9) (3,6) (7,8) (9,9)

powerful stream of water shot out of a nozzle. His idea for the ___ ___ ___ ___ ___
                                                                  (5,2) (3,6) (9,9) (2,9) (8,2)

___ ___ ___ ___ ___ ___ water gun was born!
(5,2) (8,7) (5,8) (2,3) (2,9) (8,2)

Traveling through a busy intersection is much easier than it once was. Thanks for this

goes to Garrett Morgan. He is the inventor of the first ___ ___ ___ ___ ___ ___ ___
                                                        (9,4) (8,2) (5,8) (5,4) (5,4) (1,1) (3,2)

___ ___ ___ ___ ___ ___! Also, firefighters and soldiers breathe easier in dangerous
(5,2) (1,1) (1,8) (7,1) (5,8) (7,3)

situations because of the ___ ___ ___   ___ ___ ___ ___ he invented.
                          (1,8) (5,8) (5,2)   (7,8) (5,8) (5,2) (2,3)

When you drop a letter into a ___ ___ ___   ___ ___ ___ ___
                             (4,9) (1,1) (1,8)   (4,9) (7,3) (3,6) (2,9)

___ ___ ___ ___ ___ ___ ___, remember Phillip Downing. He is the Black American
(7,8) (5,8) (1,1) (7,3) (4,9) (8,7) (6,7)

inventor who designed and patented it.

From the way John Albert Burr helped to improve the ___ ___ ___ ___
                                                    (7,3) (5,8) (3,5) (7,1)

___ ___ ___ ___ ___ to William Purvis's ___ ___ ___ that carried its own ___ ___ ___,
(7,8) (8,7) (3,5) (2,9) (8,2)   (9,9) (2,9) (7,1)   (1,1) (7,1) (2,3)

our lives have been enriched by the many creations of Black American inventors.

Name_____

Breaking Down Barriers

African American athletes have played important roles in breaking down racial barriers. Solve each problem below to learn about some famous athletes who paved the way for others. Then write the matching letter on each line to complete the sentence.

A. 19 x 8	F. 71 x 3	E. 58 x 8	N. 30 x 2	H. 85 x 5	L. 62 x 4	K. 56 x 7	B. 90 x 4	J. 44 x 9	S. 27 x 3	G. 82 x 7

O. 49 x 5	W. 74 x 3	D. 35 x 6	I. 22 x 5	T. 63 x 9	M. 41 x 6	U. 95 x 2	C. 16 x 8	R. 73 x 4	P. 68 x 5

Baseball

1. In 1947, ___ ___ ___ ___ ___ ___   ___ ___ ___ ___ ___ ___ ___ ___
   396 152 128 392 110 464   292 245 360 110 60 81 245 60
   became the first African American to play major-league baseball.

2. In 1975, ___ ___ ___ ___ ___   ___ ___ ___ ___ ___ ___ ___ ___
   213 292 152 60 392   292 245 360 110 60 81 245 60
   became the first black person to manage a major-league team.

Track and Field

3. Runner ___ ___ ___ ___ ___   ___ ___ ___ ___ ___ broke a world
   396 464 81 81 464   245 222 464 60 81
   record in the long jump at the 1936 Olympics.

4. In 1960, ___ ___ ___ ___ ___   ___ ___ ___ ___ ___ ___ ___
   222 110 248 246 152   292 190 210 245 248 340 425
   became the first American woman to win three Olympic gold medals in track and field.

Tennis

5. In 1957, tennis player ___ ___ ___ ___ ___ ___   ___ ___ ___ ___ ___ ___
   152 248 567 425 464 152   574 110 360 81 245 60
   was the first African American to play at Wimbledon, where she also won the title.

6. In 1975, ___ ___ ___ ___ ___ ___   ___ ___ ___ ___ became the
   152 292 567 425 190 292   152 81 425 464
   first African American male to win the Wimbledon title.

Run, Run, Run!

Many of the United States' best track-and-field athletes have been Black Americans. They have won medals and set record after record over the years! Use your multiplying and dividing skills to complete the activities about some of these athletes.

Part 1: Complete the chart. To convert seconds to minutes, divide by 60 and round the quotient to the nearest thousandth. To convert minutes to seconds, multiply by 60. Show your work on another sheet of paper.

Athlete	Year	Event	Time in Seconds	Time in Minutes
Jesse Owens	1935	100 yd.	9.4	
Jesse Owens	1935	220 yd.	20.3	
Wilma Rudolph	1960	100 m	11.3	
Wilma Rudolph	1960	200 m	23.2	
Carl Lewis	1984	100 m		0.165
Carl Lewis	1984	200 m		0.33
Florence Griffith-Joyner	1988	100 m	10.49	
Florence Griffith-Joyner	1988	200 m	21.34	
Carl Lewis	1991	100 m	9.86	
Michael Johnson	1996	200 m		0.322

Part 2: Complete the chart below. Multiply to change a large unit to a smaller one. Divide to change a small unit to a larger one.

400-meter relay = _____ -centimeter relay
_____ -meter race = 10,000-centimeter race
800-meter race = _____ -centimeter race
_____ -meter race = 100,000-centimeter race
10,000-meter race = _____ -kilometer race
25-kilometer race = _____ -meter race

Bonus Box: Which athlete had the best time in the 100-meter race? Write the athletes' names and times in order from fastest to slowest.

Additional Student Practice Pages

- Use the pages for independent practice.

- Use a reading passage and its corresponding comprehension questions as a group listening comprehension activity.

- Use the practice pages to gather black history facts that will be of interest to your students. Share a different fact each day during Black History Month.

- Use the pages for homework.

Name_____

A Shooting Star

Read the passage.

Grant Hill was born in Dallas, Texas. He was born on October 5, 1972. Grant grew up in Reston, Virginia. As a child, Grant learned how to play the piano. He also practiced playing basketball. Grant was a strong player for his high school team.

Grant went to Duke University. At Duke, Grant played on two championship teams. He was named the player of the year in his conference during his fourth year.

After college, Grant played for the Detroit Pistons. In 1996, he played basketball in the Olympic Games. His team won the gold medal! Grant married Tamia Washington in 1999. He also played for the Orlando Magic and the Phoenix Suns.

Grant helps people in many ways. He visits schools and reads to children. He awards money to young people who want to go to college. He gives money and time to many charities.

Find each pair of events in the passage.
Color the basketball in front of the event that happened first.

1. ◯ Grant learned how to play the piano.
   ◯ He went to Duke University.

2. ◯ Grant played basketball in the Olympic Games.
   ◯ He played basketball on his high school's team.

3. ◯ Grant lived in Reston, Virginia.
   ◯ Grant married Tamia Washington.

4. ◯ Grant played for the Detroit Pistons.
   ◯ Grant played for the Orlando Magic.

5. ◯ Grant played on two championship college teams.
   ◯ Grant was born in Texas.

George Washington Carver: The Plant Doctor

"He could have added fortune to fame, but caring for neither, he found happiness and honor in being helpful to the world."

—George Washington Carver's epitaph

Why did some plants flower in the fall, some in the spring, and some not at all? How could a tiny seed grow into a mighty oak? George Washington Carver puzzled over these questions as he went about his chores on Moses and Susan Carver's farm in Missouri.

George was born at a time when slavery was still legal. Many slaveowners treated their slaves harshly. George's owner did not think it was right to mistreat slaves. His beliefs angered the local Ku Klux Klan, who raided the Carvers' farm and took George and his mother away. The Carvers sent out a searcher on horseback to look for them. Finally baby George was found and returned. His mother, however, was never heard from again.

The Carvers raised the frail child. They taught him to read and write. George soon gained a reputation for having a "green thumb." Plants just seemed to flourish under his care. He was even nicknamed the "plant doctor"! George wanted to know more about plants. He knew he would have to leave the Carvers' farm, so he set out on a journey. He wanted to find answers to the many questions that swirled around in his head.

In the next few years George moved from one midwestern town to another. He would attend a school until that school could no longer challenge him. He would then move on to another town. George supported himself by doing laundry and other odd jobs. Life was often hard. Sometimes he barely had enough food to eat. But his thirst for knowledge never went away. When George wasn't working or studying, he was busy sketching. He loved to put on canvas the beauty that he saw around him.

Finally George was ready for college. He was very disappointed when he was turned away because of his skin color. But George did not give up his dreams. He was admitted to Simpson College in Indianola, Iowa, in 1890. Six years later, at the age of 36, he earned his master's degree in agriculture from what is now Iowa State University. His achievements with plants began to bring him fame. Booker T. Washington, a well-known Black American leader, asked George to come teach at a new school for Black Americans in Tuskegee, Alabama. George agreed. He spent the next 47 years researching plants and teaching throughout the South.

In the early 1900s the boll weevil destroyed acres and acres of cotton in the South. Many families depended on the income made from the sale of their cotton. George discovered that peanut plants were unharmed by this pest. George took the peanut and created hundreds of useful products with it. He turned peanuts and sweet potatoes into profitable staples for the South. His reputation grew. Many leaders from around the world visited his small laboratory.

In 1943 the "plant doctor" died, having made the world a much better place in which to live.

George Washington Carver: The Plant Doctor

Complete the following. Use the back of this page if you need more room for your writing.

1. Which of the following words describe George as a young boy?

   ___ curious   ___ observant   ___ lazy   ___ frail

2. What does it mean to have a "green thumb"?_____

   _____

3. Why did young George leave the Carvers' farm?_____

   _____

4. What did George love to do in his free time? _____

   What is your favorite pastime? _____

5. List one way George's life was affected by racism. (Racism is the belief that one race is

   better than others.) _____

   _____

6. George used his degree in agriculture to research and teach others about plants. What else

   might someone do with an agricultural degree? _____

   _____

7. List some important food staples grown in your state. _____

   _____

8. Number the following three events in the order in which they happened:

   ___ a. George graduated from college.

   ___ b. George was stolen from his owner by a band of raiders.

   ___ c. George began studying the many uses for peanuts.

9. Why do you think George was called the "plant doctor"? _____

   _____

10. George was born in 1860. How old was he when he died? _____

Additional Activity: Some of the products that George made from peanuts included *soup,
pickles, chili, meal, instant and dry coffee, salve, bleach, washing powder, paper, ink, plastics,
shaving cream, rubbing oil, linoleum, shampoo, axle grease,* and *synthetic rubber.* Use magazine
and newspaper pictures to make a collage of these products.

Note to the teacher: Use with the reading passage on page 52.   53

A Woman in Space

Use proofreading marks to correct ten mistakes in the passage.

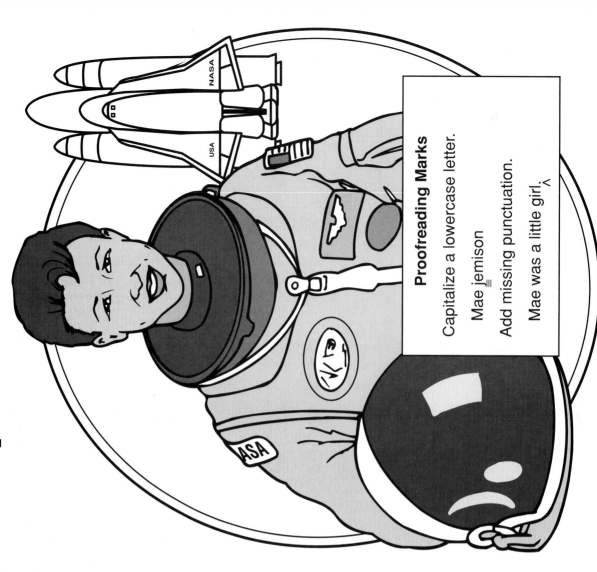

Proofreading Marks

Capitalize a lowercase letter.

Mae jemison

Add missing punctuation.

Mae was a little girl.

Mae Jemison

Mae jemison was born on October 17 1956.

She was born in alabama. In high school, Jemison thought she wanted to be an astronaut. Jemison finished school. she worked as a doctor. But Dr. Jemison still wanted to be an astronaut. In 1992, she flew on the space shuttle *Endeavour* She was the first African American woman in space.

Dr. Jemison helped start a camp for kids. It's a science camp Campers do a lot of thinking and learning.

Now dr. Jemison lives in Houston Texas. She has two cats Their names are sneeze and Little Mama.

Michael Jordan:
King of the Slam Dunk

Michael Jordan looks like a magic show on the basketball court. He seems to fly when he jumps, he runs like lightning, and he makes baskets from "impossible" places on the court. He is the king of the slam dunk.

Jordan's play is not a series of slick tricks, though. No, Jordan's magic can only be spelled out one way— H-A-R-D W-O-R-K. Here's the story of what it took for this hard-working athlete (born February 17, 1963) to become one of the best players in the NBA (National Basketball Association).

Raised in Wilmington, North Carolina, Michael Jordan spent his childhood playing sports with his brothers and friends. His father built a backyard court where the neighborhood children played almost daily. Jordan wasn't a great player then, however. In fact, he wasn't even tall for his age! His father, James Jordan, said that Michael was simply determined to win. He had to work harder to make that happen.

In high school, Jordan was a well-rounded athlete. But basketball was not his sport. As a ninth-grader, he didn't make the high school team because he was too small. In the tenth grade, he made the team but was dropped soon after the season began.

Then it happened. Jordan grew four inches between the tenth and eleventh grades. He grew another three inches in his senior year. Then, at six feet six inches, his body was a good match for all that practice. He had a winning combination at last!

After the eleventh grade, Jordan attended a special basketball camp for talented players headed for big-time college basketball. In his last year of high school, Jordan practiced an extra hour every morning at six with his coach. His game improved and he became more confident.

He won a scholarship to the University of North Carolina at Chapel Hill. He played well enough to earn the title Rookie of the Year in his conference. In the 1984 Summer Olympic Games, he led the U.S. basketball team to a gold medal. That same year he quit college and joined the Chicago Bulls, a professional basketball team in the NBA. In the pros, he was an instant success. He returned to school and completed his degree in 1986.

In his first year, Jordan led the NBA in points with a grand total of 2,313. He was named Rookie of the Year and an All-Star. He worked wonders for the Bulls' ball club. Attendance at the Bulls' home games increased 87% as fans came to see Jordan play. His "magic" continued. Jordan was awarded the title of the NBA's Most Valuable Player for the 1987–88, 1990–91, 1991–92,1995–96, and 1997–98 seasons!

So the next time you wish you had some magic to help you perform well, think of Michael Jordan. Then get to work!

Michael Jordan: King of the Slam Dunk

Answer the questions below.

1. How did Michael Jordan become one of the best players in professional basketball?_____

   _____

   _____

2. Has Michael Jordan always been successful in basketball? Why or why not? _____

   _____

   _____

3. Name two factors that helped Jordan's high school basketball career._____

   _____

   _____

   _____

4. Name three highlights of Michael Jordan's basketball career._____

   _____

   _____

   _____

5. Look up the meaning of *rookie* in the dictionary. What do you think is so special about being

   named Rookie of the Year?_____

   _____

6. Why did attendance at the Chicago Bulls' home games improve so much?_____

   _____

7. What do you think is the most important thing for an athlete to be a success?_____

   _____

   _____

8. In what sport would you like to become more skilled? What are some things that you can do to

   improve your play?_____

   _____

   _____

The Best of The Mailbox® *Black History* • ©The Mailbox® Books • TEC61174 • Key p. 77

56   **Note to the teacher:** Use with the reading passage on page 55.

Elijah McCoy (1844–1929)
Inventor

Have you ever heard the expression "It's the real McCoy"? It means "the real thing." This saying became **popular** after the Civil War because of an invention: the oil drip cup. This **tiny** container provided oil for the **essential** moving parts of heavy machinery such as train engines. When buying an oil lubricating system, businessmen would ask, "Is this the real McCoy system?" Soon the term was used by others to say something was **bona fide.**

The inventor of this device was a **bright** African American named Elijah McCoy. Elijah's parents had escaped slavery by running away to Canada on the Underground Railroad. After the Civil War, the McCoys moved to Michigan. Elijah's parents used their savings to send him to Scotland to study engineering.

When Elijah returned to the United States, he began work as a fireman on a train. He hoped to solve an industrial **hazard:** the dangerous overheating of locomotives. Trains had to stop frequently for someone to oil engine parts. This helped to **reduce** friction. Elijah invented a device that oiled engine parts as the train was moving. He received a patent for it in 1872. In 1920 he opened his own company to make and sell his **many** inventions. McCoy's **innovative** spirit is remembered today whenever someone says, "It's the real McCoy."

Recognizing Synonyms
Match each boldface word with its synonym below:

1. danger _____
2. well-known _____
3. smart _____

4. small _____
5. numerous _____
6. lessen _____

7. inventive _____
8. necessary _____
9. authentic _____

Expand Your Vocabulary
Circle the word or phrase in each group that does not belong. Circle it in the selection above. Then write a definition for that word or phrase on the back of this sheet.

1. locomotive / friction / train
2. "the real McCoy" / bona fide / patent
3. lubricating / engine / locomotive
4. danger / hazard / frequently
5. solve / device / invention
6. essential / expression / vital

Write About It!
Pretend you are a reporter investigating a crime at a local museum. An object of value (such as a painting) has been taken and replaced with a forgery. Tell why this object is not the real McCoy.

Name _____

Rosa Parks:
Mother of the Civil Rights Movement

"No," Rosa Parks replied quietly to the bus driver. "I'm not going to get up and give my seat to a white person." It wasn't the first time Rosa had felt angry about the rules which treated people differently. When she was a little girl, Rosa had hated the water fountains marked "Colored" for the blacks to use. She didn't like the old, crowded schools she attended while the white children went to new ones. Rosa disliked the fact that she could not sit down and drink a soda at the same lunch counter where white people were served. But the way blacks were treated on the city buses in Montgomery, Alabama, made Rosa angriest of all.

Black people paid their fares at the front of the bus. But then they had to get off the bus and walk to the rear to enter it. They had to sit in a special section in the back of the bus. If a white person got on the bus and found no seat, the driver would tell the black person sitting nearest the front to move and give the white person his seat.

And that's what Rosa Parks refused to do on December 1, 1955. She was tired after working all day sewing dresses and suits. "I'm not going to move," she repeated to the driver. Rosa was arrested and taken to jail.

Word about Rosa's protest spread. Blacks refused to ride the buses, and the bus company lost thousands of dollars. Rosa's lawyers went to court to prove that the bus company was not obeying the United States Constitution when it treated black people unfairly. After almost a year, the Supreme Court said that the bus company had to change its rules. Black people were allowed to enter the bus from the front and sit anywhere they chose. No one had to give up his seat.

Rosa Parks helped make a big change in our country because she was tired—tired of being treated unfairly. Her courage earned her the nickname, "the mother of the modern civil rights movement."

A court must look at the facts to make a decision. You, too, should examine the facts to make a wise decision. On your paper, draw a chart like the one shown. List the differences between the treatment of whites and blacks in 1955.

	Whites	Blacks
Schools		
Water Fountains		
Lunch Counters		
Buses		

Now compare the differences. Write a paragraph telling whether or not you think the Supreme Court made a good decision.

General Colin Powell
American Hero

"Trust me," said the general during one of his many newscasts. His manner was calm and confident. Throughout the Persian Gulf War, General Colin Powell appeared on television many times. He knew it was important for the American people to be well **informed** about the war's progress. After only 42 days, the fighting came to an end. The general's mission had been a success! Later that year, President George H. W. Bush awarded Colin the Medal of Freedom for leading our country through a difficult time.

Colin Luther Powell was born on April 5, 1937, in Harlem, a black community in New York City. His parents moved there from Jamaica in search of a better life. Colin's parents worked very hard to provide for their family, but still found time for him and his sister. Work and family were the two most important things to the Powells.

When Colin was five years old, his family moved to the Bronx, another area in New York City. There they lived in an apartment building with people from many different backgrounds—Irish, Jewish, and Italian. Colin attended school, although he wasn't a very good student. His parents urged him to study, but his lessons did not interest him.

When Colin graduated high school and began college, he did not know what he wanted to do with his life. Then one day he saw a marching drill team. As the **cadets** moved in unison in their crisp black uniforms, they caught Colin's attention. That was it! Colin would become a soldier. He joined the ROTC and eventually became the team's commander. He had direction—a goal. Colin's grades improved and he experienced a feeling of confidence and pride in his new successes.

After college, Colin joined the army and underwent rugged training courses where he learned things, such as how to parachute and survive in the wilderness. Colin's first assignment was in West Germany. His job was to protect Europe from the powerful Soviet Union. Colin also served in the war in Vietnam. He continued to do his best and prove himself to be a strong leader. He was promoted many times. He also married and began a family.

In 1972, after earning his master's degree in business administration, Colin was chosen to serve as a special assistant at the White House. People liked him. He was very organized and **dedicated.** Colin went on to become an assistant to the Secretary of Defense. In 1987, he became President Reagan's national security adviser. Two years later Colin became the first black chairman of the Joint Chiefs of Staff, supervising everyone in the armed forces. In 2001, he was appointed secretary of state.

General Colin Powell retired from the military in 1993 and left the secretary of state post in 2005. Through hard work and dedication, Colin accomplished many extraordinary things and earned many honors. He is truly an American hero.

General Colin Powell American Hero

Directions: Answer the following items. Use another sheet of paper if you need more space to write.

1. Why did General Powell hold frequent newscasts during the Persian Gulf War?

   _____

   _____

2. How do you think Colin's life in the Bronx helped shape his character? _____

   _____

   _____

   _____

3. What do you think was the turning point in Colin's life? Explain. _____

   _____

   _____

4. Name two of Powell's achievements. Describe how he accomplished them. _____

   _____

   _____

   _____

5. Tell about a goal you have achieved. How did it make you feel? _____

   _____

   _____

6. Define *informed, cadets,* and *dedicated* as used in the article. _____

   _____

   _____

   _____

   _____

   _____

   _____

   _____

The Best of The Mailbox® *Black History* • ©The Mailbox® Books • TEC61174 • Key p. 78

60   **Note to the teacher:** Use with the reading passage on page 59.

Jackie Robinson
Baseball Legend

"For enduring every taunt...and not lashing out in hate. For standing up with **dignity.** For standing up. For opening our eyes. For empowering an entire race...Thank you, Jackie Robinson." Hank Aaron, Ken Griffey Jr., and others said these words in a 1997 television commercial. They paid **tribute** to an all-time baseball great, Jackie Robinson.

Jackie Robinson has been called the best athlete ever to play major league baseball. But because he was the first black player in modern major league baseball, he also took much abuse and hatred. Some white people didn't think that black men could or should play ball in the major leagues. Jackie said, "There's not an American in this country free until every one of us is free."

Jackie was born on a small farm in Georgia in 1919. He was the fifth child of Jerry and Mallie Robinson. The family rented the land on which they lived. They paid the owner a lot of money. It was a hard life. Shortly after Jackie's birth, his father left the family. Mrs. Robinson was left destitute. Mallie and her children were given a place to live with her half brother in California.

Life in California was a struggle, but the move was a good decision. California offered more for Black Americans than the South. Schools were not segregated. There was, however, still prejudice. For example, Jackie could not swim with his friends in the city pool. Jackie was determined to use his skills as an athlete and a student to fight racial injustice. At college, Jackie became the best all-around athlete in the entire country. He did very well in basketball, baseball, football, and track!

On April 10, 1947, Jackie made it big! The Brooklyn Dodgers offered him a place on their team. Many people were angry that the Dodgers would let a black man play on their team. Others were happy and excited. Jackie answered the abuse with silence. His skill and style soon won over many more fans. Jackie became the first Black American to win a batting title, lead the league in stolen bases, play in an all-star game, play in the World Series, win a Most Valuable Player award, and gain election to the Hall of Fame. Jackie's special character and abilities in the face of racism were great strides for the **civil rights** of Black Americans.

Jackie retired from baseball in 1957. He was active in the civil rights movement until his death in 1972. Jackie was awarded the Presidential Medal of Freedom in 1986. "He struck a mighty blow for equality, freedom, and the American way of life," President Reagan said. "Jackie Robinson was a good citizen, a great man, and a true American **champion.**" Jackie never gave less than his best. Thank you, Jackie Robinson.

Jackie Robinson
Baseball Legend

Directions: Answer the following questions. Use another sheet of paper if you need more space to write.

1. Why are many professional athletes indebted to Jackie Robinson? _____
_____
_____

2. Do you agree with Jackie's statement: "There's not an American in this country free until every one of us is free"? Explain. _____
_____
_____
_____

3. Why do you think Jackie was able to fight racism with his excellence in sports? _____
_____
_____
_____

4. Jackie Robinson was a role model for many people. Tell about someone who is an important role model in your life. _____
_____
_____
_____

5. In your own words, tell why Jackie Robinson was a true American champion. _____
_____
_____
_____

6. Define *dignity, tribute, civil rights,* and *champion* as they are used in this article. _____
_____
_____
_____
_____
_____

The Best of The Mailbox® *Black History* • ©The Mailbox® Books • TEC61174 • Key p. 78

62   **Note to the teacher:** Use with the reading passage on page 61.

Marshall "Major" Taylor

Read each sentence.
Use context clues to help you circle the meaning of the boldfaced word.

1. Taylor was given the nickname Major because he wore a soldier's **uniform.**
   E. clothing   F. badge   G. armor

2. Major was thought to be one of the fastest **cyclists** in the world.
   G. runners   H. bike riders   I. drivers

3. He **forfeited** many races because of being fouled by other cyclists.
   B. won   C. lost   D. did not ride in

4. He refused to be upset by the **mind-set** of people who did not approve of his being in the contests.
   R. brains   S. sight   T. beliefs

5. He had to overcome many **barriers.**
   M. rivers   N. sounds   O. troubles

6. In 1899 this **capable** athlete set seven world records!
   E. talented   F. lazy   G. lucky

7. That same year he **conquered** the World Sprint Championship.
   W. lost   X. tied   Y. won

8. Major once rode in a **grueling** six-day race in New York.
   K. easy   L. tough   M. windy

9. After riding 1,732 miles over 142 hours, he must have been **fatigued.**
   B. scared   C. tired   D. smart

10. Some people have said Taylor's success is **comparable** to that of Lance Armstrong's.
    N. similar to   O. better than   P. different from

What did the newspapers call Marshall Taylor?
To answer the question, match the letter of each circled answer
above to a numbered line below.

"___ ___ ___   ___ ___ ___ ___ ___ ___ ___"
  4   2   1   3   7   9   8   5 10   6

Name _____

A Woman Who Made a Difference

Susie King Taylor was born a slave in 1848. She became free at age 14. Susie went on to become a teacher and nurse. She recorded some of her thoughts in a journal. Read each paragraph below to find out more about this amazing Black American. Write your answers to the questions on another sheet of paper.

1. Susie's family was owned by the Grests, a white couple with no children. The Grests were kind and loving to Susie and her brother. How do you think Susie felt when she met other white people?

2. Many slave families were separated when parents or children were sold to other owners. This did not happen to Susie's family. How do you think this affected Susie?

3. When Susie was seven, she went to live with Dolly Reed, her grandmother. Dolly cleaned homes and did laundry for others. What skills do you think she taught Susie?

4. Dolly had never learned to read. She wanted Susie's life to be better than hers. How do you think she helped Susie?

5. Susie's male relatives joined the Union Army during the Civil War. When the Union troops left the family's island home, Susie traveled with them. She did their laundry, cooked their meals, and taught them to read and write. Why do you think she did these things?

6. Susie was the first black army nurse. She served African American soldiers during the Civil War for over four years. She was never paid for her work. Why do you think Susie was willing to work so hard for no pay?

7. When smallpox broke out, Susie cared for the sickest soldier. Why do you think she did this even though she was not a trained nurse?

8. In the summer of 1863, Susie got the chance to work with Clara Barton. Clara later founded the American Red Cross. What do you think Clara thought of Susie's abilities?

Phillis Wheatley
American Poet (1753–1784)

A slim volume of poems was published in England in 1773. A young American author was pictured inside, slender and large-eyed, seated at a desk. In her hand she held a **quill** pen. Her name was Phillis Wheatley. She was America's first black poet.

Phillis Wheatley's life is believed to have begun in Senegal, Africa. At the age of about seven, she was stolen from her family. She was taken to Boston aboard the slave ship *Phillis*. Conditions aboard slave ships were horrible and the young girl barely survived the trip. In Boston, John and Susannah Wheatley bought her at a slave **auction.** Susannah named her Phillis, like the name of the ship.

Susannah was 52 and wanted a personal servant. But Phillis proved to be no ordinary child. She quickly learned to speak English. Then she learned to read and write in English and in Latin. She studied poetry and the Bible and wrote her first poem at age 14. The Wheatleys' **frail** slave girl was becoming a poet.

Phillis's poems were modeled after such writers as Alexander Pope and other neoclassical poets. Her poetry was eloquent. Phillis became widely known in Boston after writing an elegy for the famous preacher George Whitefield. She was recognized all over New England as a gifted poet.

Phillis's fame even spread to Europe. At Susannah's prompting, Phillis sailed to England in 1773 to publish her poems. Phillis's book of poems was only the second book published by an American woman. It was the first book ever published by a Black American. Phillis was only 20 years old.

While in England, news reached Phillis that Susannah's health was failing. Phillis **hastily** returned home. Susannah was very ill. Phillis cared for Susannah for a year, and during that time Phillis was given her freedom. She was no longer a slave! At the end of that year, however, Susannah died. Phillis's biggest supporter was gone.

In 1775 the American Revolution began. Americans were too busy with the war, too busy with surviving, to think much about poetry. Phillis continued to write, though, because she didn't know how to do anything else. After writing a poem about General George Washington, she was invited to meet with him in 1776. It was a proud moment for the former slave girl.

Phillis remained with John Wheatley until his death in 1778. After his death, Phillis was without a home. She married a free black man named John Peters. Phillis tried to get a second book of poems published, but there was not enough interest. Her husband was unsuccessful in business and soon was in debtor's prison.

Phillis spent her final days in a home for the poor. In 1784 Phillis wrote her last poem, "Liberty and Peace." The poem celebrated the end of the war. But Phillis never saw it in print. At 31, America's first black poet died. Phillis died alone and was buried in an unmarked grave. However, Phillis Wheatley left her mark on history. Today she is recognized as the mother of Black American literature.

Phillis Wheatley
American Poet (1753–1784)

Directions: Answer the following questions. Use another sheet of paper if you need more space to write.

1. Phillis was an extraordinary child. Support this opinion with a fact from the biography.

   _____

   _____

   _____

2. Choose an event that you think was a turning point in the life of Phillis Wheatley. Explain your choice. _____

   _____

   _____

3. Did Susannah Wheatley have a positive influence or negative influence on Phillis's life? Explain your answer. _____

   _____

   _____

4. Why do you think Phillis died alone and penniless? _____

   _____

   _____

5. Why is Phillis called the mother of Black American literature? _____

   _____

   _____

6. Define *quill, auction, frail,* and *hastily* as they are used in this article. _____

   _____

   _____

   _____

   _____

   _____

   _____

Tiger Woods
Golf Champion

Earl ran excitedly into the house to get his wife, Tida. Their son had just swung a golf club with perfect form. The most amazing thing about it was that their son, Tiger, was less than one year old! Tiger's father decided that he would help his son develop this **natural** talent for golfing. By the age of two, Tiger was already playing the game amazingly well. Tiger even appeared on television, beating a famous comedian named Bob Hope in a putting contest. People around him began to recognize that young Tiger was a champion in the making.

Tiger's real name is Eldrick. He was born on December 30, 1975. Tiger was nicknamed in honor of a friend who saved his father's life during the Vietnam War. Tiger's mother, Tida, is from Thailand. She met Earl Woods, a Black American soldier, in Thailand, while he was serving in the Vietnam War. The couple married and then moved to America after Earl left the military.

When Tiger was four years old, his father took him to a golf course to practice. It was there that Tiger met the club pro, Rudy Duran, who coached him until he was about ten years old. Tiger loved golf more than anything else. Although Tiger's parents knew he had a great future in golf, they were determined that their son would also get a good education and learn to be a responsible person. Both Tida and Earl always insisted that their son finish his homework before going out to practice his game and that he display sportsmanlike behavior.

Tiger began to win many tournaments. At the age of eight, Tiger won his first junior world championship. He went on to win four more of these titles, in addition to three U.S. Junior Amateur titles and more than 100 local junior titles. Tiger was unstoppable! As his ability grew, Tiger's parents continued to encourage him to stay positive about himself and his game.

After graduating from high school with honors, Tiger attended Stanford University on a golf **scholarship.** In 1996, Tiger became the first golfer to win three **consecutive** U.S. Amateur Championships. That same year, Tiger made a very difficult decision. He left college in order to become a **professional** golfer. In 1997, Tiger achieved a monumental goal by winning the Masters Tournament and setting tournament records. Tiger is the youngest person ever to win the tournament and the first winner of African or Asian heritage.

Tiger Woods continues to work at being the best golfer and the best person he can be, proving himself a true champion.

Tiger Woods
Golf Champion

Directions: Answer the following items. Use another sheet of paper if you need more space to write.

1. Tiger was an extraordinary child. Support this opinion with a fact from paragraph one.

   _____

   _____

   _____

2. Tiger was named after his father's friend from the Vietnam War. Do you think this proved to be a fitting nickname for Tiger? Why or why not? _____

   _____

   _____

3. How did Tiger's parents help him develop into a great champion? _____

   _____

   _____

4. Why do you think the decision to leave college was difficult for Tiger? _____

   _____

   _____

5. Write a sports headline describing Tiger's 1997 Masters victory. _____

   _____

6. Define *natural, scholarship, consecutive,* and *professional* as they are used in the article.

   _____

   _____

   _____

   _____

   _____

Bonus Box: Tiger Woods once said he would like to be the Michael Jordan of golf. What do you think he meant by this? Did he achieve his goal?

Great Beginnings

Carter G. Woodson

Frederick Douglass

In February 1926, the African American historian, Carter G. Woodson, founded *Negro History Week.* During the 1970s his idea became *Black History Week.* In 1976 the week became Black History Month, a monthlong celebration to honor the contributions of African Americans.

In the beginning, the celebration observed the birthdays of Frederick Douglass (February 14) and Abraham Lincoln (February 12). Douglass was a runaway slave who pretended to be a sailor. He escaped to New Bedford, Massachusetts. While a slave, he had been taught to read and write by his master's wife. Douglass became a public speaker who talked in favor of *abolition,* the ending of slavery. Douglass later started an antislavery newspaper while he lived in New York. He also held several government positions in Washington, DC.

Today people can visit one of Douglass's former homes in Washington, DC. It now includes the Museum of African Art and the Frederick Douglass Institute.

A. Answer the following questions on the lines provided.

1. What was the original celebration that now has become Black History Month?

   _____

2. How many years later was this celebration lengthened from one week to a month?

   _____

3. What helped Frederick Douglass become a public speaker? _____

   _____

4. Define *abolition.* _____

   _____

5. List two accomplishments of Frederick Douglass. _____

   _____

   _____

6. Why do you think Black History Month also honored Abraham Lincoln's birthday?

   _____

   _____

B. Pretend that you are Frederick Douglass. On another piece of paper, write a speech that you would give in favor of abolition. Describe your feelings about freedom and why you think slavery should end.

A Black History Mystery

In celebration of Black History Month, test your knowledge of famous Black Americans with this riddle. First decide whether each statement is true or false. Use encyclopedias and other resources to help you. Then circle the letter in either the **true** or **false** column. Write the circled letter in the blank above the matching number at the bottom of the page.

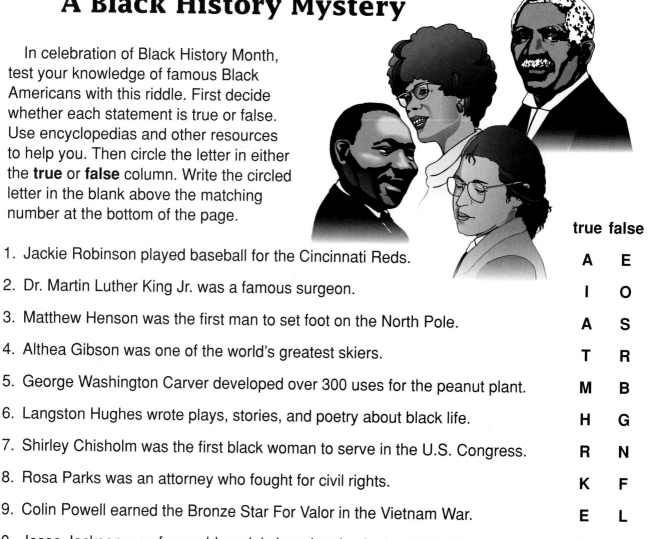

		true	false
1.	Jackie Robinson played baseball for the Cincinnati Reds.	A	E
2.	Dr. Martin Luther King Jr. was a famous surgeon.	I	O
3.	Matthew Henson was the first man to set foot on the North Pole.	A	S
4.	Althea Gibson was one of the world's greatest skiers.	T	R
5.	George Washington Carver developed over 300 uses for the peanut plant.	M	B
6.	Langston Hughes wrote plays, stories, and poetry about black life.	H	G
7.	Shirley Chisholm was the first black woman to serve in the U.S. Congress.	R	N
8.	Rosa Parks was an attorney who fought for civil rights.	K	F
9.	Colin Powell earned the Bronze Star For Valor in the Vietnam War.	E	L
10.	Jesse Jackson won four gold medals in swimming in the 1936 Olympics.	W	D
11.	Dr. Ronald McNair was the first Black U.S. Supreme Court Justice.	J	O
12.	Thurgood Marshall was a Baptist minister who ran for president in 1984.	C	T
13.	Duke Ellington was a great jazz musician and composer.	T	P
14.	Mary McLeod Bethune wrote the famous book *Roots*.	Y	O
15.	Marian Anderson was the first black soloist with the Metropolitan Opera of New York City.	D	T
16.	In 1753, Benjamin Banneker built a clock made entirely of wood.	E	C

Harriet Tubman helped slaves escape on

" __ __ __   __ __ __ __   __ __   __ __ __ __ __ __ __ __ ."
   12 6 9   7 14 3 10   13 2   8 4 16 1 15 11 5

The Best of The Mailbox® Black History • ©The Mailbox® Books • TEC61174 • Key p. 79

Note to the teacher: You may wish to divide students into pairs to complete this activity.

Name

Timeline Tips

Cut out the cards. Then use the clues below to glue the cards in the correct order on the timeline.

1874	1883	1940	1948	1977	1988

Clues:
1. Charles started storing blood plasma after Jan made his shoe machine and before Alice won at the Olympic Games.
2. Elijah got a patent for his ironing board in 1874.
3. The most recent event was Mae becoming an astronaut.
4. June studied weather before Mae became an astronaut and after Alice won her medal.

The Best of The Mailbox® Black History • ©The Mailbox® Books • TEC61174 • Key p. 79

Elijah McCoy	**Charles R. Drew**	**Alice Coachman**	**Mae Jemison**	**Jan Ernst Matzeliger**	**June Bacon-Bercey**
invented the ironing board	discovered a way to store blood plasma in blood banks	first African American woman to win an Olympic gold medal	became the first female African American astronaut	created a machine that shaped the upper part of shoes	a weather expert who made a scholarship fund for women to study meteorology

Famous Feats

Read the name of each Black American. For each ordered pair of symbols, write the matching letter from the grid. Then use this clue to help you match the person to his or her achievement.

C 1. Lena Horne

M I C R O P H O N E
(♦+) (■●)(♦▲) (♦■) (♦+) (▲■)(♦●) (♦+) (■+)(♦▲)

___ 2. Sidney Poitier

— — — — —
(♦+) (♦+) (●♦) (■●)(♦▲)

___ 3. Mae Jemison

— — — — — — —
(■■) (♦●) (▲♦) (♦■) (♦■) (●+) (♦▲)

___ 4. Jackie Robinson

— — — — & — — —
(●▲)(▲▲)(●+) (●+)   (●▲)(▲▲)(♦■)

___ 5. Langston Hughes

— — — & — — —
(▲■)(♦▲)(■+)   (■●)(■+)(▲+)

___ 6. Thurgood Marshall

— — — — —
(●●) (▲▲)(●♦) (♦▲) (●+)

___ 7. George Washington Carver

— — — — — —
(▲■)(♦▲)(▲▲)(■+)(▲♦)(♦■)

___ 8. Mary McLeod Bethune

— — — — —
(▲▲)(▲■)(▲■) (●+) (♦▲)

___ 9. Wilma Rudolph

— — — — —
(♦+) (♦▲)(■▲)(▲▲)(●+)

___10. Louis Armstrong

— — — — — — —
(♦■) (♦■)(▲♦) (♦+) (▲■)(♦▲)(♦■)

A. I was the first black U.S. Supreme Court justice.

B. Born in New Orleans, I became known as one of the world's greatest jazz musicians.

C. I am a famous black performer known for my beauty and singing of the blues.

D. In 1992, I blasted off into space on *Endeavour*, becoming the first Black American woman to accomplish this task.

E. I spent many years doing agricultural research on a special plant.

F. I was the first Black American to climb to the top of the film industry as a leading man.

G. I was a Black American educator who fought to improve opportunities for blacks.

H. I was a Black American author, best known for my poetry.

I. When I joined the Brooklyn Dodgers in 1947, I became the first Black American to play major-league baseball.

J. After overcoming being partially crippled by polio, I won three gold medals in the 1960 Olympics.

▲	A	B	C	D	E
●	F	G	H	I	J
+	K	L	M	N	O
■	P	Q	R	S	T
♦	U	V	W	X	Y/Z

▲ ● + ■ ♦

Two Famous Black Americans

Circle the adverb in each sentence.
(Hint: Adverbs tell how, when, or where.)

Colin Powell

1. As a soldier in the United States Army, Colin Powell had to travel anywhere the army needed him.

2. He received a medal when he bravely pulled several men from a burning helicopter.

3. He did well in the military, rising to the rank of four-star general.

4. He successfully led the United States military during Desert Storm.

5. Recently, Colin Powell has been the Secretary of State.

Serena Williams

6. As a champion tennis player, Serena Williams often wins the matches in which she plays.

7. Many of her tennis matches are played outside.

8. In 1999, Serena happily won, for the first time, a professional match against her sister.

9. She proudly won a gold medal for the United States in the 2000 Olympics.

10. In 2002, she played skillfully enough to be named the number one player in the world.

Bonus Box: On the back of this sheet, write three sentences about another famous Black American. Circle the adverbs in your sentences.

Black Americans in the News

These newsworthy Black Americans are making headlines!
Help Rhea Porter get her newspaper ready for print by following
the directions below.

Directions: Study each photograph. Find the matching
headline. Write the letter of the corresponding photograph in
the blank. Then decide in which newspaper section the headline
belongs. Color the newspaper by the code.

(A) Shirley Franklin	(B) Tiger Woods	(C) Mae Jemison	(D) Benjamin Carson
(E) Savion Glover	(F) Colin Powell	(G) CeCe Winans	(H) Vonetta Flowers
(I) Venus and Serena Williams	(J) Dale Emeagwali	(K) Denzel Washington	(L) Condoleezza Rice

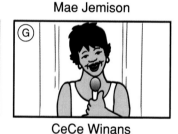

1. _____ Sisters Win Tennis Championship

2. _____ Gospel Singer Wins Eighth Grammy Award

3. _____ New Mayor of Atlanta Wins by a Landslide

4. _____ Surgeon Performs History-Making Operation

5. _____ President Selects First Black Secretary of State

6. _____ First Black American Woman Launched Into Space

7. _____ Young Tap Dancer Wins Tony Award for Broadway Show

8. _____ Woman Receives Scientist of the Year Award for Cancer Research

9. _____ President Selects First Black Female National Security Adviser

10. _____ Golfer Becomes Youngest Player to Win Major Championship

11. _____ Bobsledder Becomes First Black American Winner of Winter Olympic Gold

12. _____ Star Becomes Second Black American to Win Oscar for Best Actor

Color Key
entertainment = yellow
government = blue
science = green
sports = red

Answer Keys

Page 8

1. parents
2. born
3. was
4. Minty
5. was
6. night
7. Underground
8. escape
9. adult
10. thankful
11. freedom
12. people

POSTAGE STAMP

Page 9

1. Harriet wouldn't pretend to be polite just so she could get a job as a house slave. She never pretended to be satisfied with her life as a slave. She could not be forced to smile when she worked. She risked her life to help a runaway slave.
2. She helped other slaves escape to freedom on the Underground Railroad.
3. The Underground Railroad was a system for helping slaves escape to freedom.
4. Answers will vary.
5. Answers will vary.
6. Answers will vary.

Page 17

1. fairly
2. laws
3. peaceful
4. boycott
5. money
6. marches
7. speeches
8. hard

Page 18

Answers may vary. Possible answers include the following:

1. A
2. C
3. B
4. C
5. A
6. A
7. B
8. C
9. B

Bonus Box: Answers will vary.

Page 19

1. Dr. King is born in Atlanta, Georgia, in 1929.
2. Dr. King graduates from college in 1948.
3. Dr. King graduates from the seminary in 1951.
4. Dr. King marries Coretta Scott in 1953.
5. Dr. King becomes pastor of Dexter Avenue Baptist Church in 1954.
6. Dr. King earns a doctoral degree in June 1955.
7. Dr. King leads a bus boycott beginning in December 1955.
8. Dr. King gives his "I have a dream" speech in 1963.
9. Dr. King is awarded the Nobel Peace Prize in 1964.
10. Dr. King is shot and killed in 1968.

Page 20

Answers may vary. Possible answers include the following:

1. Dr. King's dream was that all people would be treated the same.
2. Years ago, black people and white people could not use the same bathrooms. They had to go to different schools.
3. We celebrate Dr. King's birthday because he worked to make sure that blacks and whites were treated fairly. He helped to solve problems in a peaceful way.
4. Answers will vary.
5. Answers will vary.

Page 21

1. O
2. F
3. O
4. F
5. F
6. O
7. F
8. O
9. O
10. F

Bonus Box:
Possible answers include the following:

1. It is hard
3. harder
6. liked
8. most important
9. best

Page 22

1. fought
2. lived
3. went
4. led
5. changed
6. gave
7. came
8. won
9. marked
10. was

MAHATMA GANDHI

Page 23

1. "my mother said I was as good as anyone," Dr. King told a friend.
2. Dr. King said, "everyone can be great."
3. Dr. King told his followers, "if pushed, do not push back. if struck, do not strike back."
4. "hate cannot drive out hate," he stated. "only love can do that."
5. Dr. King said, "love builds up and unites; hate tears down and destroys."
6. "I can't be silent," Dr. King explained. "I am a citizen of the world."
7. "sooner or later, all the people of the world will have to discover a way to live together," he declared.
8. Dr. King said, "love is the key to the problems of the world."
9. "This is our hope," he told the crowd.
10. He stated, "we cannot walk alone."
11. "we cannot turn back," Dr. King advised.
12. Dr. King declared, "I have a dream today!"

Page 24

1. 1968 − 1929 = 39
2. 39 × 15 = 585
3. 585 ÷ 5 = 117
4. 711
5. 711 × 12 = 8532
6. 8532 ÷ 4 = 2133
7. 2133 − 29 = 2104
8. 2104 ÷ 4 = 526
9. 1052
10. 1052 − 136 = 916
11. 916 + 31 = 947
12. 1894
13. 1984
14. 1984 − 1 = 1983

The year that Martin Luther King Jr.'s birthday became a national holiday was 1983.

Page 25

$\frac{1}{2}$ $\frac{2}{4}$	$\frac{3}{5}$ $\frac{2}{3}$	$\frac{1}{4}$ $\frac{3}{12}$	$\frac{12}{30}$ $\frac{2}{5}$	$\frac{9}{10}$ $\frac{16}{20}$
powerful	everyone	in	without	Remember
$\frac{1}{6}$ $\frac{5}{30}$	$\frac{6}{8}$ $\frac{3}{4}$	$\frac{4}{16}$ $\frac{8}{32}$	$\frac{24}{32}$ $\frac{2}{4}$	$\frac{2}{7}$ $\frac{2}{14}$
and	It is	history,	freedom	sword
$\frac{2}{3}$ $\frac{9}{18}$	$\frac{3}{2}$ $1\frac{1}{2}$	$\frac{3}{6}$ $\frac{10}{24}$	$\frac{15}{21}$ $\frac{5}{7}$	$\frac{6}{4}$ $1\frac{1}{4}$
together	a	when	wounding....	children
$\frac{3}{10}$ $\frac{6}{20}$	$\frac{8}{10}$ $\frac{4}{5}$	$\frac{14}{28}$ $\frac{3}{7}$	$\frac{18}{32}$ $\frac{9}{16}$	$\frac{6}{36}$ $\frac{1}{6}$
just	weapon	reaches	It is	that
$\frac{4}{3}$ $1\frac{1}{3}$	$\frac{5}{25}$ $\frac{2}{5}$	$\frac{9}{12}$ $\frac{3}{4}$	$\frac{2}{6}$ $\frac{3}{18}$	$\frac{18}{2}$ 9
weapon.	peace	which	marches	heals.
$\frac{31}{5}$ $6\frac{6}{6}$	$\frac{10}{4}$ $2\frac{1}{2}$	$\frac{1}{11}$ $\frac{3}{33}$	$\frac{1}{8}$ $\frac{64}{8}$	$\frac{72}{10}$ $7\frac{2}{5}$
equal.	unique	cuts	a	always.

"Nonviolence is a powerful and just weapon. It is a weapon unique in history, which cuts without wounding....It is a sword that heals."

Page 26

O. 1929
F. 15
H. 1953
T. 1958
E. 5
N. 1963
A. 1964
C. 39
I. 1968
R. 1986

THE CONTENT OF THEIR CHARACTER

Page 27
Answers will vary.

Page 28
Answers may vary.

1929 — born
1930s — grew up in Atlanta, Georgia
1935 — began school
1948 — received first college degree
1951 — received second college degree
1953 — married Coretta Scott
1954 — became a pastor in Montgomery, Alabama
1955 — helped set up the Montgomery bus boycott
1956 — bus law changed
1957 — helped found an organization to help black people
1962 — met with President Kennedy
1963 — gave famous speech, "I have a dream"
1964 — received Nobel Peace Prize

Page 45
A. Vonetta Flowers (red)
B. Colin Powell (green)
C. Benjamin Carson (blue)
D. Condoleezza Rice (green)
E. Denzel Washington (yellow)
F. Tiger Woods (red)

Page 47

Lonnie Johnson was working on one of his many inventions. He wanted to create a **heat pump** that didn't harm the environment. Suddenly, a powerful stream of water shot out of a nozzle. His idea for the **Super Soaker** water gun was born!

Traveling through a busy intersection is much easier than it once was. Thanks for this goes to Garrett Morgan. He is the inventor of the first **traffic signal**! Also, firefighters and soldiers breathe easier in dangerous situations because of the **gas mask** he invented.

When you drop a letter into a **big blue mailbox**, remember Phillip Downing. He is the Black American inventor who designed and patented it.

From the way John Albert Burr helped to improve the **lawn mower** to William Purvis's **pen** that carried its own **ink**, our lives have been enriched by the many creations of Black American inventors.

Page 48

A.	152	O.	245
F.	213	W.	222
E.	464	D.	210
N.	60	I.	110
H.	425	T.	567
L.	248	M.	246
K.	392	U.	190
B.	360	C.	128
J.	396	R.	292
S.	81	P.	340
G.	574		

1. JACKIE ROBINSON
2. FRANK ROBINSON
3. JESSE OWENS
4. WILMA RUDOLPH
5. ALTHEA GIBSON
6. ARTHUR ASHE

Page 49

Athlete	Time in Seconds	Time in Minutes
Jesse Owens	9.4	**0.157**
Jesse Owens	20.3	**0.338**
Wilma Rudolph	11.3	**0.188**
Wilma Rudolph	23.2	**0.387**
Carl Lewis	**9.9**	0.165
Carl Lewis	**19.8**	0.33
Florence Griffith-Joyner	10.49	**0.175**
Florence Griffith-Joyner	21.34	**0.356**
Carl Lewis	9.86	**0.164**
Michael Johnson	**19.32**	0.322

400-meter relay = **40,000**-centimeter relay
100-meter race = 10,000-centimeter race
800-meter race = **80,000**-centimeter race
1,000-meter race = 100,000-centimeter race
10,000-meter race = **10**-kilometer race
25-kilometer race = **25,000**-meter race

Bonus Box: Carl Lewis
1. Carl Lewis, 9.86 sec.
2. Carl Lewis, 9.9 sec.
3. Florence Griffith-Joyner, 10.49 sec.
4. Wilma Rudolph, 11.3 sec.

Page 51

1.
2.
3.
4.
5.

Page 53

1. *curious, observant,* and *frail*
2. Being able to get plants to grow and thrive.
3. George left the farm to attend school.
4. George loved to draw in his free time.
5. Answers may vary and may include that George was separated from his mother because of racism. He also was not allowed to attend a college because of his skin color.
6. Answers will vary.
7. Answers will vary.
8. The correct order is a: 2; b: 1; c: 3.
9. He could make sick plants well.
10. George was 83 years old when he died.

Page 54

Mae Jemison

Mae jemison was born on October 17, 1956. She was born in alabama. In high school, Jemison thought she wanted to be an astronaut. Jemison finished school. she worked as a doctor. But Dr. Jemison still wanted to be an astronaut. In 1992, she flew on the space shuttle *Endeavour*. She was the first African American woman in space.

Dr. Jemison helped start a camp for kids. It's a science camp. Campers do a lot of thinking and learning.

Now dr. Jemison lives in Houston, Texas. She has two cats. Their names are sneeze and Little Mama.

Page 56

1. Answers will vary.
2. No, he did not make the high school team when he was in the ninth grade, and he was cut from the team in the tenth grade.
3. Answers may vary and may include that he grew taller and he practiced very hard. He attended a special basketball camp.
4. Answers will vary.
5. *Rookie* means a novice or beginner.
6. More and more fans come to see Michael Jordan play.
7. Answers will vary.
8. Answers will vary.

Page 57
1. danger: *hazard*
2. well-known: *popular*
3. smart: *bright*
4. small: *tiny*
5. numerous: *many*
6. lessen: *reduce*
7. inventive: *innovative*
8. necessary: *essential*
9. authentic: *bona fide*

Expand Your Vocabulary
1. locomotive/(friction)/train: *friction*—the rubbing of one thing against another
2. "the real McCoy"/bona fide/(patent): *patent*—a document that provides legal protection to an inventor, securing the exclusive right to make, use, or sell an invention
3. (lubricating)/engine/locomotive: *lubricating*—applying a material such as grease or oil to moving parts to reduce friction
4. danger/hazard/(frequently): *frequently*—often
5. (solve)/device/invention: *solve*—to find a solution, explanation, or answer for
6. essential/(expression)/vital: *expression*—a significant word or phrase

Write About It!
Answers will vary.

Page 58
Answers will vary.

Page 60
1. He wanted Americans to know about what was happening.
2. Answers may vary and may include that he learned to get along with people from many different backgrounds and understand that despite ethnic differences, all people are equal.
3. Answers may vary and may include when he joined the ROTC. It gave him a goal and helped him experience confidence and success.
4. Answers will vary.
5. Answers will vary. Accept reasonable responses.
6. In the article, *informed* means having information, being educated about something; *cadets* means young people who are training to become members of the armed forces; and *dedicated* means giving a lot of time and energy to something.

Page 62
1. He paved the way for racial integration in professional sports.
2. Answers will vary.
3. Answers may vary and may include that since a black player was able to do well at America's great pastime, more doors were opened to other minorities.
4. Answers will vary.
5. Answers will vary and may include that Jackie Robinson stood and fought for equality and freedom, virtues highly valued by Americans.
6. In the article, *dignity* means the quality of being worthy or esteemed; *tribute* means a gift or compliment given to another; *civil rights* means rights of equality for all people; and *champion* means one who fights for others' rights or honor.

Page 63
1. E
2. H
3. C
4. T
5. O
6. E
7. Y
8. L
9. C
10. N

THE CYCLONE

Page 64
Answers will vary.

Page 66
1. Answers will vary and may include that Phillis was an extraordinary child because she survived the horrible conditions of becoming a slave. She then went on to quickly learn the English language, to learn to read and write in English and Latin, to study poetry and the Bible, and to write her first poem at age 14.
2. Answers will vary.
3. Answers will vary.
4. Answers will vary and may include that Phillis was alone because John and Susannah Wheatley had died. Phillis was poor because the American Revolution had turned away people's interest from poetry and her husband had been a poor businessman, ending up in debtor's prison.
5. Answers will vary.
6. *Quill* means a hollow, stiff feather used as a pen; *auction* means a sale of property to the highest bidder; *frail* means fragile, physically weak; *hastily* means hurriedly or quickly.

Page 68

1. Answers will vary and may include because he was swinging a golf club when he was less than a year old, he played golf amazingly well by the age of two, and he beat an adult in a putting contest.
2. Answers will vary and may include that Tiger's nickname is fitting because he is a fierce competitor and he is courageous.
3. They helped him develop his natural talent, encouraged him to be positive about himself and his talent, and made sure that he had a good education.
4. Answers will vary and may include that it was difficult because he would not earn his degree and would have to earn a living playing golf.
5. Answers will vary.
6. In the article, *natural* means present from birth rather than being learned; *scholarship* means a grant or a prize that pays you to go to college or to follow a course of study; *consecutive* means happening or following one after the other; and *professional* means making money for something others do for fun.

Bonus Box: Answers will vary.

Page 69

1. Negro History Week
2. 50 years later
3. While a slave, he had been taught to read and write by his master's wife.
4. Abolition is the ending of slavery.
5. Answers will vary and may include that he started an antislavery newspaper, he held government positions in Washington, DC, and he was a public speaker.
6. Answers will vary and may include that on January 1, 1863, President Abraham Lincoln issued the Emancipation Proclamation, a historic document that led to the end of slavery in the United States.

Page 70

1. false—**E**
2. false—**O**
3. true—**A**
4. false—**R**
5. true—**M**
6. true—**H**
7. true—**R**
8. false—**F**
9. true—**E**
10. false—**D**
11. false—**O**
12. false—**T**
13. true—**T**
14. false—**O**
15. true—**D**
16. true—**E**

Harriet Tubman helped slaves escape on "THE ROAD TO FREEDOM."

Page 71

1874	1883	1940	1948	1977	1988
Elijah McCoy	Jan Ernst Matzeliger	Charles R. Drew	Alice Coachman	June Bacon-Bercey	Mae Jemison
invented the ironing board	created a machine that shaped the upper part of shoes	discovered a way to store blood plasma in blood banks	first African American woman to win an Olympic gold medal	a weather expert who made a scholarship fund for women to study meteorology	became the first female African American astronaut

Page 72

1. C; m i c r o p h o n e
2. F; m o v i e
3. D; s h u t t l e
4. I; b a l l & b a t
5. H; p e n & i n k
6. A; g a v e l
7. E; p e a n u t
8. G; a p p l e
9. J; m e d a l
10. B; t r u m p e t

Page 73

1. As a soldier in the United States Army, Colin Powell had to travel (anywhere) the army needed him.
2. He received a medal when he (bravely) pulled several men from a burning helicopter.
3. He did (well) in the military, rising to the rank of four-star general.
4. He (successfully) led the United States military during Desert Storm.
5. (Recently), Colin Powell has been the Secretary of State.
6. As a champion tennis player, Serena Williams (often) wins the matches in which she plays.
7. Many of her tennis matches are played (outside).
8. In 1999, Serena (happily) won, for the first time, a professional match against her sister.
9. She (proudly) won a gold medal for the United States in the 2000 Olympics.
10. In 2002, she played (skillfully) enough to be named the number one player in the world.

Page 74

1. I, sports (red)
2. G, entertainment (yellow)
3. A, government (blue)
4. D, science (green)
5. F, government (blue)
6. C, science (green)
7. E, entertainment (yellow)
8. J, science (green)
9. L, government (blue)
10. B, sports (red)
11. H, sports (red)
12. K, entertainment (yellow)

Index of Black American Achievers

A

Aaron, Hank, 46
Anderson, Marian, 41, 70
Angelou, Maya, 41
Armstrong, Louis, 40, 72
Ashe, Arthur, 48

B

Bacon-Bercey, June, 71
Banneker, Benjamin, 70
Bearden, Romare, 42
Bethune, Mary McLeod, 35, 46, 70, 72
Bluford Guion, Jr., 41
Brooks, Gwendolyn, 32, 33
Burr, John Albert, 47

C

Carson, Benjamin, 44, 45, 74
Carver, George Washington, 32, 33, 36, 52–53, 70, 72
Chamberlain, Wilt, 46
Chisholm, Shirley, 35, 70
Coachman, Alice, 32, 33, 71
Coleman, Bessie, 32, 33
Cosby, Bill, 36
Crumpler, Rebecca Lee, 46

D

Douglass, Frederick, 35, 69
Downing, Phillip, 47
Drew, Charles Richard, 37, 71

E

Ellington, Duke, 46, 70
Emeagwali, Dale, 74

F

Flowers, Vonetta, 44, 45, 74
Franklin, Shirley, 74

G

Gibson, Althea, 38, 48, 70
Glover, Savion, 74
Griffith-Joyner, Florence, 49

H

Henson, Matthew, 32, 33, 37, 46, 70
Hill, Grant, 51
Horne, Lena, 72
Hughes, Langston, 30, 35, 70, 72

J

Jackson, Jesse, 38, 70
Jemison, Mae C., 32, 33, 46, 54, 71, 72, 74
Johnson, Lonnie, 47
Johnson, Michael, 49
Jordan, Michael, 55–56

K

King, Coretta Scott, 26, 28, 37
King, Martin Luther, Jr., 10–28, 46, 70

L

Lewis, Carl, 49

M

Marshall, Thurgood, 32, 33, 37, 46, 70, 72
Matzeliger, Jan Ernst, 71
McCoy, Elijah, 57, 71
McNair, Ronald, 70
Morgan, Garrett, 38, 40, 47

O

Owens, Jesse, 41, 48, 49

P

Paige, Satchel, 32, 33
Parks, Rosa, 41, 46, 58, 70
Poitier, Sidney, 72
Powell, Colin, 43, 45, 59–60, 70, 73, 74
Purvis, William, 47

R

Rice, Condoleezza, 43, 45, 74
Robeson, Paul, 38
Robinson, Frank, 48
Robinson, Jackie, 36, 48, 61–62, 70, 72
Rudolph, Wilma, 46, 48, 49, 72

T

Taylor, Marshall, 63
Taylor, Susie King, 64
Truth, Sojourner, 36
Tubman, Harriet, 4–9, 32, 33, 46, 70

W

Washington, Booker T., 32, 33, 41
Washington, Denzel, 44, 45, 74
Wheatley, Phillis, 65–66
Williams, Daniel Hale, 32, 33
Williams, Serena, 73, 74
Williams, Venus, 74
Winans, CeCe, 74
Winfrey, Oprah, 32, 33, 40
Woods, Tiger, 44, 45, 67–68, 74
Woodson, Carter G., 69